TERRARIUM CRAFT

TERRARIUM CRAFT

Create 50 Magical, Miniature Worlds

BY Amy Bryant Aiello & Kate Bryant

PHOTOGRAPHY BY Kate Baldwin

Timber Press

PORTLAND / LONDON

Photography by Kate Baldwin.

Published in 2011 by Timber Press, Inc.

The Haseltine Building
133 S.W. Second Avenue, Suite 450
Portland, Oregon 97204-3527
www.timberpress.com

2 The Quadrant
135 Salusbury Road
London NW6 6RJ
www.timberpress.co.uk

Printed in China
Design by Nicki Brandt

Library of Congress Cataloging-in-Publication Data
Bryant Aiello, Amy.
Terrarium craft : create 50 magical, miniature worlds /
Amy Bryant Aiello & Kate Bryant ;
photography by Kate Baldwin. -- 1st ed.
p. cm.
Includes bibliographical references and index.
ISBN 978-1-60469-234-1
1. Terrariums. 2. Glass gardens. I. Bryant, Kate. II. Title.
SB417.B79 2011 635.9'824--dc22
A catalog record for this book is also available from the British Library.

THANKS TO MY HUSBAND, MICHAEL,
for his love and support and my daughter, Chiara Lucia, for just being.
Special thanks to family and friends and to Martha Bergman-Gamblin
and Katie Bailey who have been so helpful.

—Amy Bryant Aiello

MY GRATITUDE TO FRIENDS AND FAMILY
who sustained me with beautiful meals, cups of tea, and love.

—Kate Bryant

TABLE OF CONTENTS

PREFACE

Making a terrarium involves taking elements of nature and arranging them in a way that is exquisite—a collage with nature. It's like capturing the experience of walking in the forest and looking down to see a breathtaking organic arrangement, or spotting an ideal composition in sand, foam, and driftwood on the beach. A terrarium is a snapshot of that perfect array of natural elements, somehow contained yet still wild at the core.

Artemisia, our shop in Portland, Oregon, is a space for me to play, both on a broad scale (the shop is one big, constantly changing installation) and within the confines of the individual terrariums. Plants, shells, stones, crystals, and other natural materials are innately beautiful—we hardly need to do anything to them at all—just spending time in their presence brings out the artist in all of us.

For me, a terrarium is like a secret home inside a home. I often layer materials in the terrariums, showing what is below the surface; like dreams are to our daily lives, something that lives underneath and has a separate reality of its own. Once I begin working on a design, I start to think about making terrariums when I go to sleep and when I wake up—I feel the excitement of the muse! I wish that for you as well.

—Amy Bryant Aiello

INTRODUCTION

Our natural world is filled with boundless beauty, from the most delicately random arrangements of bark, moss, and lichen on the forest floor to graceful heaps of seaweed, driftwood, and shell tossed up on a beach. In this book, you will learn how to distill the beauty of these natural elements into artful terrariums.

The fifty terrariums shown in these pages—loosely grouped by inspiration into forest, beach, desert, or fantasy—incorporate a range of fascinating components, including plants, lichen, moss, crystals, stone, sand, and shells. Every project contains a materials list, as well as detailed instructions for composing and caring for the terrarium (all of which builds on the practical information covered in the first part of the book). And while each of the compositions is beautiful enough to be worth recreating, they were really designed to inspire—to serve as catalysts to ignite your own creativity and personal vision. Far from being meticulously planned, they were made with what artist Amy Bryant Aiello had available at her shop at the time the book was created. Even the process of making them was intuitive, if not somewhat spontaneous—pieces were added, swapped out, and gently prodded until they looked right, even during the photo shoot. The idea is to play with the materials and enjoy the process itself, while accepting the delicious imperfection of it.

A walk in the woods, along a beach, or through a dry canyon would be ideal for getting in an experimental frame of mind. Natural scenery—wind-tossed sand, tawny beach grass, or mossy rocks—is the best inspiration for creating these terrarium collages. In essence, making a terrarium really begins with your own relationship with nature. As you gather your materials, let them guide your creative process. Start with materials you love, keep an open mind, and allow them to take you somewhere unexpected. The beauty already exists—you are the curator, selecting which pieces will be included and assembling them in a way that delights you.

Once made, set your terrarium where you can enjoy and observe it. If you aren't a gardener or even if you think of yourself as a "brown thumb," you can find living plants that are easy to care for—or captivating dried mosses and lichens that require no attention at all, save for admiration. Add a significant personal memento and a terrarium can even be a kind of altar, encapsulating dreams, passions, and memories. Simple to care for yet highly expressive, such terrarium designs bring the natural world closer to home—and us closer to nature.

PRACTICAL
MATTERS

A helpful primer on all things terrarium, this comprehensive section covers material choices, plant care information, and general terrarium-making techniques and tips. Before you embark on a terrarium project, take some time to read about the many types of glass containers, the various substrates, and the complementary materials including stones, shells, crystals, moss, lichen, architectural plants, and miscellaneous embellishments. Besides your own patch of nature and local shops, the resource section (page 188) contains a list of places to purchase materials. Always check local, state, and federal regulations before collecting any natural materials—and take only what you need.

CONTAINERS

It all begins with the container. A terrarium needs to be clear glass, not only so you can admire the contents but also so any plants inside can absorb needed light. Aside from these obvious practicalities, the glistening and reflective qualities of the glass itself are an essential part of the beauty of the modern terrarium.

Terrarium glassware can be found in a nearly infinite variety of sizes and shapes. Good terrarium containers can be repurposed canning and pickle jars, cookie jars, old bottles, glass cloches and cake trays, wine and beer glasses, and many other types of household glassware.

Glass can readily be found in places ranging from your own kitchen cabinets or recycling bins to thrift stores, yard sales, florists, boutiques, crafting shops and websites, and kitchenware and home décor stores.

Simple glass receptacles are usually best for showcasing the kinds of terrariums in this book. Fussier or more ornate glass can sometimes distract from the subtleties of form that are found in natural materials.

It's sometimes practical to first pick the glassware—the most prominent part of your design—and let it guide your choice of materials. But there's nothing wrong with starting with your materials and simply seeing where they take you. The pleasure of the whole process often lies in that experimentation.

When applicable, container dimension details in this book are recorded as height x width x depth. Don't worry if you aren't able to find containers with the exact dimensions of those shown. You will likely be making substitutions anyway—which is ok!—and might just discover an even better glass container and materials mix while you're at it.

CLOCKWISE FROM BACK LEFT: tall, skinny vase, large bubble bowl, stemmed votive glass (inside bubble bowl), large teardrop (hanging in backdrop), French canning jar, lidded apothecary jar, small teardrop, large and small pyramid vases, small bud vase, cloche on tray, science jar.

Size

In terms of size, nearly anything can work, from the tiniest spice jar on up. The size of the container matters—not only for the plants and other materials inside but also when your living space is limited. Consider where the terrarium will go, then measure the "footprint" of the glass you intend to use to make sure it will fit. This is particularly important if you need to place your terrarium on a narrow ledge, sill, or shelf.

If space isn't an issue, you can let your imagination run wild. It's fun to start with a big, spacious container if you haven't made a terrarium before: the options for materials are greater, and temperatures within the terrarium will be more moderate and air flow better. There's also a greater margin for error if you forget to water your terrarium or if it sits in too hot a spot one afternoon. By the same token, the smaller the terrarium, the smaller the margin of error—the plants will have less root space so lack of water can be more problematic, and a small enclosure will heat up faster if accidentally left in direct sun.

Shape and lids

Your own personal aesthetic is the best guide to finding an inspiring form for your terrarium. Whether you like the look of a curvy glass teardrop, a modern glass cube, a recycled glass jam jar, or something else entirely, there are numerous styles and shapes to choose from.

Should the container be open or closed? Fifteen minutes of direct summer sun on a closed terrarium can be lethal to a living plant within it—even a succulent—so be sure to keep a lidded terrarium's top off unless it's out of any direct sun. A closed, lidded terrarium also keeps humidity inside. If you plan to maintain a closed terrarium, choose plants that will relish this humidity and stagnant air. Try ferns, tropical houseplants, and mosses. Avoid placing air-plants, orchids, or succulents in this environment, as they are not likely to thrive for long without fresh, buoyant air.

THE FOUNDATION: SOIL, SAND, AND GRAVEL

Soil, sand, or gravel is the substrate, or foundation, of the terrarium. Choosing the right foundation is important, not only from a visual perspective (setting up a pleasing contrast or harmony with the other terrarium materials) but also for achieving conceptual accord. Whether your terrarium is inspired by the forest, the sea, the desert, or some fantastical world, the substrate you choose will play a supporting role.

Planting mixes

Plants have to grow in *something*, after all. Most potted plants come with enough soil in their pots to thrive in your terrarium but if you're starting with cuttings or very small plants—or if the plants' roots have filled up the pot and there's little soil left for the roots—you may find you need to add a bit more planting mix. The plants you select will determine the type of planting mix (if any) you need.

DIY MIXES

Dry mix for cacti and succulents.
Most succulent plants, including cacti, require a fast-draining soil mix containing lots of horticultural-grade sand and grit. A typical cactus and succulent mix would be composed of two-fifths sterilized compost (screened garden compost or commercial compost), one-fifth horticultural-grade sand, and two-fifths grit (usually horticultural pumice, perlite, or gravel or lava fines). You can also just buy small, pre-mixed bags of cactus and succulent potting soil.

Mixes for moisture-loving plants.
Many houseplants such as begonias and peperomias appreciate good drainage as well but a high-quality commercial potting mix works fine. Most quality blends consist of approximately one-third compost, one-third peat or coir, and one-third pumice or perlite. Avoid potting soil with added wetting agents or fertilizers and always be sure to follow the particular plant's specific care recommendations about watering. Carnivorous plants need an acidic, very moisture-retentive soil mix. For these plants, blend equal parts peat moss and horticultural-grade sand.

Sand

Given the variations in local geology around the world it only makes sense that different sands and minerals are commercially available depending on where you live. That said, it is possible to order almost anything from almost anywhere. See what's available at local craft and terrarium shops, decorative rock stores, pet and aquarium shops, landscaping suppliers, and sand, gravel, and stone retailers. If local resources are limited, start widening your search on the internet.

Naturalistic terrariums look best with subtly colored sands, such as glistening white quartz sand, warm-toned speckled Monterey beach sand, sparkly gray-black hematite sand, and reddish-purple garnet sand, as well as a range of other beautiful sands. Never harvest beach sand, as salt is lethal to plants. And beware of artificially dyed and colored sands, which can look harsh and, well, artificial.

Since your container may not be exactly the same dimensions as the containers pictured, be mindful when adding sand. Use your judgment and eye. Sometimes it helps to roughly approximate the ratio of materials to one another when purchasing materials and purchase a little more sand than you think you'll need. Large containers can absorb a surprising amount of sand and it's better to be generous than to skimp on materials.

CLOCKWISE FROM TOP LEFT: pure quartz sand, hematite sand, Monterey beach sand, garnet sand.

IN THE SANDBOX

Garnet sand.
A fine-grained, dark, reddish-purple almandine garnet sand sometimes sold as Emerald Creek Garnet.

Hematite sand.
A fine-grained, glistening, gray-black sand composed mainly of iron oxide, sometimes sold as Spectralite.

Monterey beach sand.
A slightly coarser sand of quartz, feldspar, and granitic rock with a warm tan color, composed of a diversity of colored granules. Buy it washed, screened, and kiln-dried so it is safe for plants.

Pure quartz sand.
A fine-grained, creamy-white silica sand that is readily available.

Gravel, stone, rocks, and pebbles

Gravel, pebbles, and stone from all over the world are available online but start your search locally. Depending on where you live, your own garden could yield interesting and worthy rock specimens. Keep your eyes open and poke around a bit. Remember that the stone needs to look as lovely dry as it does wet.

You may be able to obtain materials such as Monterey beach pebbles, small white pebbles, and crushed lava rock at gravel and rock yards or at garden and terrarium-making shops. Look for river rocks and polished rocks at rock yards, as well as gem marts where jade and specialty speckled rocks can also be found.

CLOCKWISE FROM TOP LEFT: petrified wood and agate shards, mixed river rocks, Monterey beach pebbles, polished black river rocks, green river rocks, Mexican river rocks, white pebbles (center).

ON THE ROCKS

Crushed lava rock.
A readily obtained, rusty reddish-brown, rough granular volcanic rock.

Monterey beach pebbles.
A warm, tan-colored blend of small pebbles made up primarily of multicolored quartz, feldspar, and granitic rock.

Petrified wood and agate shards.
Beautiful multicolored fossilized remains of wood (usually infused with silicate such as quartz) and agate which form when the materials are buried under sediment and preserved.

River rocks.
Smooth, matte, or polished rocks in a wide range of colors and sizes: black river rock (gray to black, various sizes); green river rock (pale green, large); Mexican river rock (gray, dark grayish-black, or ivory with a reddish cast, small); white river rock (ivory-white, large).

Speckled rocks.
These rocks resemble birds' eggs—there are many types, usually one-off finds among bins of other rocks.

Tiny mixed polished stones.
Often available in mixes of various colors and types or in consistent batches of the same color and type of mineral. Easy to purchase by the handful, bag, or pound.

White pebbles.
Small, somewhat smooth, ivory white stones with a tumbled look.

CREATING THE SCENE: SHELLS, CRYSTALS, AND MORE

The possibilities of materials permutations are truly endless. When selecting materials for terrariums, keep scale in mind—but don't be afraid to use large materials that stick out of the bowls and vases. Many materials look best when not contained but rather spilling out: flower stalks rising above rims, twigs overreaching their boundaries, special stones or pieces of handmade art dangling from twine. Feel free to experiment.

As always, check local, state, and federal regulations before collecting materials—and take only what you can use.

Shells

Seashells are a lovely addition to a terrarium—their sensuous forms and subtle colors and textures are a delight to admire up close. The best shells are the empty ones you find on a trip to the beach: instead of stuffing them into a box in your basement, arrange them in a terrarium where they can be appreciated every day. If you don't have any found shells, you can buy beautiful nautilus, conch, or mixed shells (as well as sea urchins and sea fans) at your local terrarium shop, online, or at shell purveyors. Be aware that it's the rare perfect, whole shell that is sustainably harvested: chances are, if it's intact, it was harvested with a living sea creature inside.

MATERIALS ON WOOD, CLOCKWISE FROM TINY MIXED SHELLS (IN TRAY, TOP): green sea urchins, mixed white seashells, small purple shells, tiny bronze shells (in bowl), red abalone. Materials on sea fan, clockwise from nautilus shell (top left): fig shells, striped fox shell, small white limpets, peach-striped snail shell, small sand dollars.

SEEING SHELLS

Bronze shells.
Small, univalve shells often sold by the handful or by the pound.

Fig shells.
Somewhat fragile, pear-shaped shells with a yellowish or whitish background marked with reddish-brown. They are often found in sandy, offshore areas of the Indo-Pacific Ocean.

Limpets.
Small, rock-dwelling animals that affix themselves to shoreline rocks. Shell color and shape varies by species from white to brown to tortoise shell patterns.

Mixed shells.
A diverse mix of subtly-colored, small seashells from various univalve species. Many blends of tiny seashells can be found, both on the beach if you're lucky or purchased by the scoopful.

Nautilus.
Smooth, coiled shell, lined with mother of pearl, found in tropical waters of the Indo-Pacific Ocean. Coloration varies with species. Sometimes sold cut, with the beautifully chambered interior visible.

Red abalone.
Flattened, oval-shaped shells with an iridescent interior often found on rocks near the ocean shores. The outer shell of red abalone has reddish-brown striping.

Sea fan.
Fan-shaped, dried corals found throughout the oceans of the world, particularly in the tropics and subtropics. Natural colors range from creamy whites to pinks, reds, and black, although they are also dyed in dozens of colors.

Sea urchins.
Small, spiny, round ocean animals. Depending on species, shell colors include black and dull shades of green, brown, pink, purple, and red.

Small sand dollars.
The skeletons of several species of sea urchin are usually found in sandy, shallow water of the southeastern United States, Australia, and the Caribbean.

Snail shell.
A peach-striped shell which, along with a variety of beautiful miscellaneous shells, can be found or purchased online.

Striped fox shell.
A soft-orange-striped shell.

Crystals

With their magnificent forms and jewel-tone colors, crystals are beautiful additions to miniature landscapes. Their crystalline structure and the way they are cut often helps capture light and create a sparkle and reflectivity that can bring the whole terrarium to life. In addition to the natural beauty and diversity of the crystals themselves, it can be interesting to learn about the metaphysical and healing properties assigned to the different minerals.

Every part of the world has its own geological specialties and some crystal is locally abundant and not to be found elsewhere. Find out if there is any crystal type local to your area that will be a significant addition to your terrarium. Or just purchase the crystal you find most beautiful or symbolically valuable.

CLOCKWISE FROM TINY QUARTZ CRYSTALS (IN SILVER BOWL OF HEMATITE SAND): aragonite, celestine, tiny mixed polished stones, citrine point, large quartz crystal point, cut Mexican geode, pyrite stones, selenite rose, selenite shards (small and large), vanadinite on barite, spirit quartz (center).

THE SPARKLE FACTOR

Agate or carnelian agate.
A fine-grained, waxy-looking microcrystalline quartz (silica), often with bands or stripes. Carnelian agate is usually reddish-orange.

Aragonite.
A carbonate mineral that can be white, red, yellow, orange, green, blue, or brown.

Celestine or celestite.
A delicate, icy-looking crystal composed of strontium sulfate.

Citrine points.
Color varies from pale yellow (rare, natural citrine) to reddish-yellow (much more common, usually commercially heat-treated).

Clear calcite crystals.
A clear crystal formed of common elements of sedimentary rock, particularly limestone.

Double cube pyrite in matrix.
Unusual cubic pyrite crystals are comprised of crystals of iron sulfide in a sedimentary limestone or sandstone matrix. They are found in Northern Spain.

Geodes or Mexican geodes.
Rocks with cavities lined with often-crystalline minerals such as quartz and sometimes calcite crystals that can be clear, white, or very colorful. Geodes are often cut in half so the beautiful, crystalline interiors can be seen.

Glass pebbles.
Clear glass pebbles (usually melted mineral) are readily found in garden centers and decorative rock shops.

Herkimer diamonds.
Double-terminated quartz formations named for their brilliance and diamond-like form. First mined in Herkimer, New York, but since discovered in other locations around the world.

Quartz crystal points.
Shard-shaped pieces of quartz (silicon dioxide) that are colorless and translucent. Quartz is the second-most abundant mineral on the Earth's crust and there are many colored varieties. Tiny quartz crystal pieces can also be bought by the handful, bag, or pound.

Raw pyrite stones or iron pyrite.
An iron sulfide with a rough, sparkly gold surface. Also known as "fool's gold."

Raw fluorite rocks or fluorspar.
Composed of calcium fluoride and occurring in a range of colors such as pink, purple, blue, yellow, green, red, brown and white, or clear.

Rose quartz.
A pale pink to rose-red quartz with a milky opacity.

Selenite rose.
A beautiful natural material comprised of selenite crystals (gypsum) infused with sand that forms a silky-surfaced, apricot-colored rosette with lighter, whiter edges. Usually found in arid environments.

Selenite pieces or shards.
A glassy, crystallized form of gypsum composed of hydrous calcium sulfate. The shards can vary greatly in size and can be clear to slightly opaque.

Spirit quartz.
A lovely pinkish-purple-tinted type of quartz found in South Africa.

Vanadinite.
Typically bright red to orange and sometimes gray to brown, vanadinite is composed of lead chlorovanadinite and is a dense, brittle mineral, usually found in the form of hexagonal crystals. Due to the lead content, it is important to exercise care when handling vanadinite, particularly for children. Vanadinite crystals are sometimes found on white barite, often originating in Morocco.

Miscellany of muses

The tiny world tucked within a terrarium is partly a representation of your creative efforts but also—at least when you're working with natural materials—an expression of the essential beauty or charm of the materials themselves.

Some of these materials—pieces of tree root and wood, seedpods, stones, old bottles and marbles, animal bones, teeth, and feathers—can be found in your own garden. Search among your own possessions, perhaps even family hand-me-downs or heirlooms, to find a plethora of materials such as unworn items of jewelry, tiny ornaments, old marbles or game pieces, and china animals. You might find silk flowers, costume jewelry, and little decorative birds at craft stores, thrift shops, and garage sales. And still more materials, from kitsch to exquisite handmade crafts, are waiting to be discovered while traveling.

Once you start making terrariums, you often develop an eye for idiosyncratic materials. A walk past a thrift shop—much less your neighbor's recycling bin—might never be the same! And the same goes for walks on the beach, in the garden, and in the woods—ideas can be found everywhere and the repertoire is limitless.

SO MANY UNIQUE MATERIALS, SO LITTLE TIME: hand-dyed and hand-spun wool, gold thread, a manzanita (*Arctostaphylos manzanita*) branch, a tiny bird, Grandma's brooch, maple (*Acer* species) samaras, a sheep jaw bone, glass bubbles, a ceramic deer figurine, ammonite (fossilized nautilus shell), a dove egg, found feathers (pheasant, blue heron, and turkey), bracket fungus, small bones, a decoration made from an old book.

NATURAL MATERIAL IDEAS

- Driftwood, twigs, and branches
- Gnarled and cleaned rose roots
- Seedpods of maples (known as "samaras" or "helicopters"), magnolias, and other trees and flowers
- Emu, chicken, and dove feathers
- Small and large animal bones and teeth
- Deer antlers
- Bracket fungus (also known as "conks")
- Dried bugs
- Ornamental grass flower stalks

NON-NATURAL MATERIAL IDEAS

- Fish hooks
- Small and medium clear glass bubbles
- Handmade paper decorations and old books
- Variously sized old bottles
- Small decorative birds and silk flowers
- Gold and silver hoop earrings and sparkly old brooches
- Old theater light bulbs
- Vintage bronze beads and French flower beads
- Porcelain trinkets, brass candleholders, and hand-carved Mexican houses
- Jute twine, gold thread, and vintage string

PLANTS AND PLANT CARE

A vast selection of beautiful plants are well suited to life in various types of terrariums—whether damp and shady, dry and desert-like, or anything in between. Choosing a plant that is compatible to the terrarium can make the difference between a terrarium that looks great for just two months and one whose living occupants flourish for years before they need to be transplanted or replaced.

Unless you need an extra large feature plant for a more expansive container, you'll probably be looking for plants in 2- to 4-inch pots. Opt for plants that are filling their pots with a healthy network of roots and inspect plants carefully for insects (they usually congregate around new growth) before introducing them into a terrarium. It can be challenging to eradicate insects once they are colonizing a terrarium plant.

The living plant materials incorporated in terrariums in this book are succulents, airplants, carnivorous plants, mossballs planted with small houseplants, mosses, and lichen. There are four main variables involved in caring for a terrarium with living plants:

- Light
- Moisture
- Fertilization
- Humidity/air circulation

Terrariums that flourish over time usually contain slow-growing plants appropriate to the medium in which they're planted, the humidity of the container, the site in which they're set, and the level of care you're able to provide.

A fairly open terrarium planted with succulents, airplants, or mosses can last indefinitely if well cared for. But don't fret if some component dies—go with the flow. If the dead material looks good, just leave it. Sometimes a light green moss will turn honey-golden and look lovely. Succulents, however, rarely look good when they pass to the other side—and airplants are famous for taking a long time to show signs of stress so they can seem to die overnight.

You get to decide how it will be in your terrarium, whether you're a careful planner and want to select just the right plants and environment or just want to make something beautiful and see what happens. But sometimes, you just have to try it and see what happens.

Succulents

Succulent plants have fleshy leaves or stems that allow them to survive prolonged periods of drought in their native habitats. In an ideal world, you'd obtain the full botanical name (genus and species) of any plant you add to a terrarium so you can learn how best to care for it. But in truth, most of the succulents commonly sold in mixed, unlabeled trays in shops are fairly straightforward in their requirements.

Most succulent and cactus plants appreciate plenty of water in summer, less in winter, and always like to dry out between waterings, whatever the time of the year. A general summer watering rule—for succulents growing indoors in bright, indirect light or a morning of sunlight and normal household temperatures—is about 1/4 to 1/2 cup every 7 to 10 days for a 2-inch plant and about 1/2 to 3/4 cup every 7 to 10 days for a 4-inch plant. In winter, water the same amount but every 10 to 14 days, or when the soil dries out to the touch. Always feel the soil before watering. If it's time to water and the soil surface feels dry to the touch, then water. Beware, however, of overwatering, as a terrarium has no drain holes. Once you've added water, you can't take it out.

Succulents usually grow in summer and rest in winter but exceptions do exist—a few succulent plant species thrive on the opposite schedule and rest in summer instead of winter. Generally, succulent plants can be fertilized with a weak solution of balanced fertilizer during the growing season (usually, spring and summer).

Most succulent plants prefer full sun but not all of them—haworthias and gasterias often grow in the shade of taller plants or rocks that help shield them from the strongest rays of the sun. It's also important to remember that a terrarium concentrates heat, which can burn plants. Keep an eye on your plants and watch for elongated growth (indicating insufficient light); brown or crisp foliage, especially tips (indicating burning); shriveled leaves (indicating insufficient water); or rotten roots (caused by overwatering).

Normal household temperatures are fine for most succulents. And while sealed terrariums are not suitable habitats for succulents, as moisture and heat tend to build up within, succulents are fairly adaptable to the lower air circulation of a terrarium with a small opening. Just be sure to keep the terrarium out of direct summer sunlight and provide proper drainage.

FAIRY WASHBOARD PLANT (*Haworthia limifolia*) IS AN INTENSELY TEXTURED SUCCULENT.

Airplants

These pineapple relatives are known as airplants because they do not root into soil. Instead, these denizens of warm climates cling to trees, rocks, telephone wires, or anything that keeps them suspended where they can receive abundant humidity, breezes, and sunshine, along with occasional drenching rain. Even though they look similar, there are many kinds, with different floral and foliar shapes and colors, and sometimes, even slightly different requirements. Learning the proper names of any airplant you add to your terrarium will help you care for it so that it doesn't just survive but actually thrives. In general, however, airplants are adaptable and basic care instructions will keep them healthy.

The best airplants for terrariums are tillandsias. They can be placed just about anywhere indoors for a month or so without harm. But to keep a tillandsia healthy over the long term, you need to provide fresh air, bright natural light, and humidity or moisture. An ideal situation for a tillandsia is to be suspended so it receives maximum bright yet indirect sunlight, air circulation, humidity (such as in a bathroom or sometimes steamy kitchen), and fertilization. Some species, particularly those with a silvery cast to the foliage, can tolerate direct sun and some drought, as long as they are positioned in a humid area or properly soaked from time to time.

To water: submerge tillandsias every 1 to 2 weeks for an hour or up to 8 hours or so (overnight). Misting is helpful in very dry conditions but cannot make up for regular soaking. Some tillandsias are especially sensitive to hard water, chemicals, or pollution in water. Distilled, bottled, or rainwater is sometimes recommended when misting or soaking.

Fertilize by misting recently soaked plants with a dilute solution of high nitrogen fertilizer such as 30-10-10. Choose a fertilizer with a non-urea–based nitrogen, as urea cannot be absorbed by airplants (urea-free formulas are often available through orchid retailers). You can also add fertilizer directly to the soaking water.

THE BULBOUS AIRPLANT (*Tillandsia bulbosa*) IS ALMOST FLOATING IN THIS TERRARIUM.

Carnivorous plants

Carnivorous plants such as pitcher plants (*Sarracenia* species), Venus flytraps (*Dionaea muscipula*), and angry bunny plants (*Utricularia sandersonii*), are mystique-evoking creatures of the highest order. They obtain nutrients through the insects they trap, thus potentially eliminating the fertilization requirement of their care. However, if there are no flies or other insects in your home, you might drop an occasional insect into the trap.

Carnivorous plants prefer very bright light when grown indoors. But, unless the terrarium is very large and open, even these sun-loving plants can burn in hot sun so be careful to pull terrarium out of direct sun in summer.

Since carnivorous plants grow naturally in bogs, their roots must be kept wet at all times. Drip water over potting soil at least once a week, depending on the light and temperature conditions in which the terrarium sits.

Some carnivorous plants are especially sensitive to hard water, chemicals, or pollution in water. Distilled, bottled, or rainwater is sometimes recommended for watering.

Often overlooked is the fact that carnivorous plants need a winter rest period—something they do not receive in the typical home. After about two years indoors, they typically stop flowering and begin to decline. If the plants are suited to your climate, plant them outdoors or, at the very least, give them a period of winter dormancy in a cool garage or near a cool basement window before returning the terrarium to its customary spot at the start of the growing season.

A WELL-KNOWN CARNIVOROUS PLANT—THE VENUS FLYTRAP (*Dionaea muscipula*).

Plants in mossballs

Mossballs are made using a Japanese bonsai technique in which plants' roots are meticulously wrapped in a ball of soil and moss. Mossballs are a wonderful way to display houseplants like cane-type begonias, peperomias, and ferns. It's generally best to select plants with similar requirements to the moss they're planted in so that both plants will thrive together. Mossballs are an easy, elegant way of bringing a lush, tropical, or foresty look into a terrarium while—if cared for well—skirting problems with mold and rot.

Care is easy: about once a week, remove the mossball from terrarium and thoroughly soak under tap. Then let the mossball sit, half submerged, for 10 to 15 minutes before returning it to the terrarium. Most plants in mossballs like to dry out slightly between waterings so lightly squeeze the mossball to test for moisture and water just as it begins to feel dry. Add a quarter-strength dilute solution of balanced fertilizer to the soaking water during spring and summer when plants are growing.

A VARIETY OF PLANTS IN MOSSBALLS ON THE LUSH SHELVES OF ARTEMISIA.

Moss and lichen

The soft, cushiony, textural component of moss and lichen provides a beautiful contrast with the sharper elements in a terrarium. The addition of vibrant colors is also invaluable: ranging from the naturally bright green of moss and yellowish-green of lichen to dyed and preserved reindeer moss which is available in shades like chartreuse, cream, pink, or black.

Approximately 12,000 species of moss exist, growing in nearly every part of the world, mostly in shady, damp, low-lying areas. If you order moss online, it could be a locally abundant species native to the vendor's area—or a species shipped from somewhere else. If you'd like to use native moss or would just rather harvest your own, be sure to obey all local, state and federal laws regarding the collection of natural materials. If you're harvesting, even from your own yard, make sure it is not a rare or endangered species. And take only what you need. Outdoors, mosses are often slow-growing and can take years to grow back so be careful to only remove chunks so that the remaining pieces can regrow.

Lichen is actually a symbiosis between a fungus and algae. The most common living lichens used in terrariums are the beard lichens (*Dolichousnea longissima* and *Usnea* species), most of which grow in humid environments. Lichen is usually collected from tree branches and rocks, and typically sold freshly harvested or dyed and preserved. As with moss, obey all collection laws and be sure to avoid rare or endangered species.

Although some species of moss and lichen resent being in urban environments, most require little care beyond consistent moisture and humidity. Test moisture level with your fingers and mist whenever moss or lichen begins to feel dry—approximately one spritz per week. Mosses and lichens—particularly lichens—can be sensitive to pollution and chemicals. Most prefer acidic conditions so if your tap water has high pH (hard or alkaline water), you may wish to use distilled, bottled, or rain water. Some species dry out and easily spring back to life upon receiving water but others are less tolerant of such fluctuations.

Provide moss and lichen with bright but indirect light: it can be a challenge to maintain them for long in a terrarium that receives direct sun or too much shade. Moss and lichen will sometimes expire if their particular water and light needs are not met. Some mosses dry to an exquisite honey-green color. Others turn brown and, if you don't like the look, you may want to replace it. Dyed reindeer moss needs no special care, as it is not a living material.

CLOCKWISE FROM PINK REINDEER MOSS: mood moss, chartreuse reindeer moss, cream reindeer moss, black reindeer moss, old man's beard lichen, feather moss.

FLUFFS, PUFFS, CLUMPS, AND MATS

Beard lichen (*Usnea* species) and old man's beard lichen (*Dolichousnea longissima*).
This soft, greenish-tan strand lichen is today mostly found in the forests of the Pacific Northwest of the United States. It is very sensitive to pollution.

Feather moss (*Ptilium* species).
Also known to gardeners as plume moss or boreal forest moss, this common type of northern hemisphere mountain moss forms dense, light green mats on rocks, rotten wood, and peaty soil.

Mood moss (*Dicranum* species).
Called mood moss by florists but known to gardeners by various epithets (depending on species) including rock cap moss, broom moss, and fork moss. These shade-loving mosses are harvested all over the country but in nearly all species are lush, velvety green, and densely clumping.

Reindeer moss (*Cladonia rangiferina*).
Actually a species of ground-dwelling lichen native to the eastern seaboard of the United States and some points west. Reindeer moss forms pillowy colonies in sandy woodland and forest margins. For the floral industry, it is dyed and preserved as pink, chartreuse, cream, black, and many other colors.

TYPES OF TERRARIUMS

Each of the terrarium types covered in this book tends to use a slightly different palette of materials. Planting techniques are also different—plants that go into dry and wet terrariums are planted directly into sand or soil, while plants in mix-it-up terrariums are kept in their pots and simply slipped into moss or lichen nests.

Dry

Dry terrariums typically have sand or pebble foundations and contain succulent plants that appreciate drying out between watering. The succulents' root balls are planted directly in the sand. Most of the dry terrariums are accompanied by instructions to scrape away the top layer of soil before planting so the potting soil does not show on the surface of the sand or pebbles. When you scrape away the top surface of soil, you are replacing it with a mulch of sand or gravel so that the plant ends up at the same level at which it was growing in its pot. The goal is to avoid planting too deeply or shallowly, as either condition can cause problems over time.

Wet

A wet terrarium contains carnivorous plants planted in potting soil, mosses, or lichen; or moisture-loving houseplants planted in mossballs. Mold and rot issues are averted—and the concomitant fussing with layers of charcoal (a material often used in terrariums)—by keeping houseplants' roots within mossballs rather than planted in potting soil without drain holes.

Mix-it-up

These terrariums blend succulent and dry-loving plants with woodsy, moisture-loving plants. This may be done successfully by keeping the succulent plants in their own pots so that they drain properly in spite of being planted in moss or lichen.

Non-living

Living plants are not imperative to a satisfying terrarium. If you're not willing or able to care for living plants, create one with dried plants and other materials. Dry seedpods and flowerheads, preserved lichen, dried moss, and twigs need no care and look beautiful with stones, sand, wood, shells, and a multitude of other natural and non-natural materials.

ASSEMBLING YOUR TERRARIUM

Making a terrarium is a pretty low-tech endeavor but you'll want to gather any necessary materials before you start. A few tools will come in handy:

- **A small jar for pouring sand into the terrarium**
- **Old chopsticks or another kind of stick for shifting hard-to-reach items**
- **A small, soft pastry or paintbrush for contouring sand and brushing any wayward sand out of plant crevices**
- **A work tray to contain materials**
- **Watering tools: a small spritzer bottle for moss and lichen, a turkey baster or narrow jar for precision watering, and a measuring cup for other plants**
- **A bowl for soaking your airplants (or just use a sink basin)**

The day before making your terrarium, thoroughly water plants so the roots hold together but are not too wet. Soak airplants for 1 to 8 hours and spritz any living mosses and lichens. Allow foliage to dry completely before working on the composition, as sand and other materials will stick to even slightly damp leaves.

Make sure to inspect all plants that you plan to add to the terrarium. First, check for any sign of insects on the plants, particularly on the new growth tips. Wash leaves carefully if any are spotted. If the infestation looks serious, replace the plant with a disease-free specimen. Also, remove any shriveled or damaged leaves.

Always clean the terrarium glass inside and out before beginning to plant. When you're ready to get started, set up a work area on newspaper or in a tray. If you are making a suspended terrarium, you can either hang it before assembling or set it somewhere while working on it. If you do the latter, first hook the twine or thread through the glass and make sure the length is suitable. Set the glass on a soft washable pillow or on a stand of some kind so that it stays in the position in which it will hang.

The two step-by-step designs that follow helpfully illustrate some essential terrarium-making techniques.

LET'S GET VISUAL

How to make a mix-it-up terrarium

NO. 1
Assemble your materials

NO. 2
Pour sand into terrarium

NO. 3
Give container a shake or two to level sand

NO. 4
Loosen moss clump, without actually separating pieces

NO. 5

Drop loosened moss clump down into container and arrange so fluffy pieces are facing up and out

NO. 6

Form a hole in moss toward the center for potted plant

NO. 7

Add small pieces of reindeer moss

NO. 8

Arrange rocks by sliding them down the sides of the terrarium

NO. 9

Add sea urchins against glass

NO. 10

Slip potted plant into hole in center of moss

NO. 11

Add remaining reindeer moss to conceal pot

NO. 12

Voila—done!

LET'S GET VISUAL

How to make a dry terrarium

NO. 1
Assemble your materials

NO. 2
Pour sand into mason jar
(not terrarium) to add later

NO. 3
Remove plant from pot and scrape
off top layer of pebbles or soil

NO. 4
Lower plant into terrarium

NO. 5
*Settle and arrange plant
in terrarium*

NO. 6
*Pour sand from mason jar into
terrarium, using your hand to keep
sand off plant and direct flow of
sand to outer edges*

NO. 7
*With sand filled in around potting
soil, give terrarium a single gentle
shake to smooth surface and lift
plant until potting soil level is just
below surface*

NO. 8
*Add pebbles to your liking over
a section of sand, maybe with a
handful scattered on the other side*

NO. 9
*Add small bunches of reindeer moss
between plant and pebbles*

NO..10
Place first stone

NO. 11
Place second stone

NO. 12
Voila—another terrarium planted!

AND FINALLY, BEFORE YOU GO…

Life and death.

Though it may be hard to imagine while making it, a terrarium probably isn't destined to live forever. Some last for years; others are temporary installations, whether due to attrition, plants outgrowing their allotted spaces, or your own changing sensibilities. Some plants can be a bit technically challenging to switch (unless they're left in their pots) but most elements can be swapped out as the mood strikes. Tiny worlds can be vulnerable places and death happens. It's part of life.

Let go.

When making your terrarium, take a slightly laissez-faire approach: drop things in and see how they land. If you like it, leave it. If you don't, take a brush or chopstick and move it around until it does something you like. It's a bit like planting bulbs in the garden—let things fall out of your hands and just tweak them if you don't like how they land.

FOREST
TERRARIUMS

EXOTIC LANDSCAPE

Suggesting **penjing** *(the Chinese art of "tray scenery") without exactly being penjing, this tiny, artful landscape relies on the transition provided by the small, shiny, round stones between the flat silver surface of the tray and the soft, puffy moss rising from it. When the gently curving cloche is removed, the atmosphere—both physical and aesthetic—is transformed.*

1 GLASS CLOCHE (16 INCHES TALL)

1 ROUND VINTAGE SILVER TRAY (14-INCH DIAMETER)

6 CUPS MOOD MOSS (*Dicranum* species)

35 SMALL PYRITE STONES

5 LARGE PYRITE STONES

1 CUP CLEAR GLASS PEBBLES, SMALL AND LARGE

1 GLASS BUBBLE

1 GNARLED ROSEBUSH ROOT, CLEANED

1 MOSSBALL WITH 'BLOODY MARY' PEPEROMIA AND 'VARIEGATA' PEPEROMIA

2 CUPS SMALL BLACK RIVER ROCKS

2 CUPS MEDIUM BLACK RIVER ROCKS

Tip

You may have to find a generous friend with a garden in order to obtain a rosebush root. Actually, any small shrub will do, as long as the root has character.

1. Clean terrarium glass inside and out.

2. Place a layer of mood moss chunks flat over the central surface of the tray, leaving 1 to 3 inches at the margins fairly clear.

3. Arrange pyrite stones (small and large) in the cracks between mood moss chunks and along outer edges of moss.

4. Place glass pebbles, small and large, along the edges of the tray and tuck glass bubble into a sweet spot between the moss and stone.

5. Nestle rosebush root atop moss to one side, and mossball planted with peperomias toward the center.

6. Take handfuls of black river rocks and scatter along margins—if too much of the tray seems obscured, push some rocks aside or remove as needed.

Care

The moss and peperomias appreciate similar conditions: warm temperatures, moist but not saturated soil, a bit of humidity (such as is found in a closed terrarium), and filtered bright light—much like a tropical rainforest floor. Place cloche some distance from a sunny window or in a window receiving no direct, hot sun in summer. Mossball may be soaked in a bowl of water for 10 to 15 minutes on a weekly basis. Once a month, add quarter-strength balanced fertilizer to soaking water. Peperomia plants should dry slightly between watering—but not enough to wilt. Squeeze mossball gently to feel for moisture.

DUSKY ANGEL

Crunchy and soft: the beauty of this terrarium lies in the simple contrast between these two qualities. Angular rose quartz pebbles comprise a solid base for the soft, earthy mossball planted with a cane-type begonia sporting dark, burgundy-tinted, slightly shiny foliage.

1 GLASS CANNING JAR WITH LID (18 INCHES TALL)
8 CUPS ROSE QUARTZ PEBBLES
1 MOSSBALL WITH ANGEL WING BEGONIA

1. Clean terrarium glass inside and out.
2. Pour rose quartz pebbles into jar.
3. Place mossball planted with begonia inside jar.

Care

Provide medium to bright, indirect light and be sure to pull terrarium out of hot, midday sun, particularly in summer. Soak mossball for 10 to 15 minutes every week or two, depending on whether top is kept closed or open.

Tip

Begonias appreciate humidity but pop the lid regularly to freshen the air. And be sure to open lid if jar receives any direct sun or the begonia will cook.

NOBODY HOLDS A CANDLE TO YOU, DEAR!

When this pitcher plant is in bloom, look out—the chartreuse flowers and the chartreuse reindeer moss make a captivating combination. Below the carnivorous plant: a bucolic vignette of herbivorous deer grazing upon reindeer moss. (Ironic juxtapositions can be fun!)

1 ROUNDED RECTANGULAR GLASS VASE
(22 X 12 X 5 INCHES)

6 CUPS SMALL BLACK RIVER ROCKS

1 YELLOW PITCHER PLANT (*Sarracenia flava*)
IN BLOOM (4- OR 6-INCH POT)

2 HANDFULS GREEN RIVER ROCKS

6 HANDFULS CHARTREUSE REINDEER MOSS

1 SET BRASS BUCK AND DOE CANDLEHOLDERS
(OR OTHER TRINKET)

1. Clean terrarium glass inside and out.

2. Layer bottom of container with small black river rocks.

3. Unpot the pitcher plant and settle into terrarium, spreading out soil mix across whole surface of terrarium and spreading plant's roots into soil.

4. Drop green river rocks around edges of glass.

5. Add handfuls of chartreuse reindeer moss and set brass candleholders into moss.

Care

Pitcher plants appreciate bright light but no direct, hot afternoon sun, which would be intensified in this glass terrarium. A warm, humid environment with constant moisture at the roots is ideal. Water with distilled or rain water. No fertilizer is necessary if the plant is trapping insects. If not, you can deliver meals by dropping insects into the trap. But don't overdo it—one bug per week is plenty.

Tip

When the pitcher plant goes dormant in winter and the flowering stems shrivel, you can light taper candles. Brown or green would look especially fine. You may not be able to track down the deer-shaped candleholders, but Bambi can be found in many other forms.

PITCHERS AT AN EXHIBITION

Looking a bit like a scientific exhibit from a Victorian plant-collecting expedition, this lovely design permits a close-up view of the unique qualities of the magnificent pitcher plants. Behold their ingenious arsenal for trapping insects—from the nectar-like secretions on the lip of the pitchers to the tiny hairs within the pitchers that prevent the insect's escape.

2 RIMMED CYLINDERS (12 INCHES TALL)
2 PITCHER PLANTS (*Sarracenia* species)
CHOPSTICKS
CARNIVOROUS PLANT SOIL MIX FROM PLANTS' POTS
1/2 CUP ROSE QUARTZ PEBBLES
1/2 CUP MONTEREY BEACH PEBBLES

1. Clean terrarium glass inside and out.

2. Remove each plant from pot and drop into glass cylinder.

3. Using a chopstick, gently tamp soil so that it is level and there are no air pockets. Scrape topmost surface of soil (about 1 inch) away from top of root ball.

4. Top dress with rose quartz in one terrarium and Monterey beach pebbles in the other. Pour in just enough water to clean up any stray soil on the glass and moisten plants' roots.

Care

Pitcher plants have specific but fairly easy requirements: plenty of sun; wet, acidic, nutrient-poor soil; and clean, pure water. In the summer, 6 to 8 hours a day of sun is best—since terrarium glass concentrates heat, pull plants away from window during hottest weather. Using distilled or rainwater for best results, apply about 1/2 cup of water per week or more as needed to keep soil wet (never allow pitcher plants to dry out). No need to fertilize: carnivorous pitcher plants obtain nutrients by capturing and digesting insects. If there are no fruit flies or other tiny insects in your home, pick up crickets from a pet shop (or capture your own insects) and drop one bug per week into pitchers.

In winter, position pitcher plants in a cooler environment so that they receive a winter rest (dormancy). During this time, their leaves slowly die back. If proper winter rest is provided, pitcher plants will produce unusual, bell-like, yellow or red flowers in spring.

Tip

Pitcher plants are available in a wide variety of colors and patterns. Mail-order nurseries that specialize in carnivorous plants will have the best selection.

MIDNIGHT TROPICALE

Resembling a black sand beach on a desert island, this creation is dark, handsome, and a little bit mysterious. The silver squill (Ledebouria socialis) resembles a little palm tree, the black begonia conjures up a tropical shrub, and the black reindeer moss could almost be washed-up detritus. The scattered pieces of fool's gold or pyrite—a name derived from the Greek word for "fire" due to its brightness and because it can be used to strike sparks—offer glistening salvation to this dusky oasis.

1 GLASS BOWL (4 X 12 INCHES)

1 'BLACK FANCY' BEGONIA (4-INCH POT)

1 SILVER SQUILL (*Ledebouria socialis*) (4-INCH POT)

8 CUPS PURE QUARTZ SAND

6 CUPS HEMATITE SAND

3 HANDFULS BLACK REINDEER MOSS

12 SMALL RAW PYRITE STONES

1 DOUBLE CUBE PYRITE IN MATRIX

1. Clean terrarium glass inside and out.

2. Remove the begonia and silver squill from their pots. Keeping the plants' root balls intact, scrape off topmost surface of soil so it doesn't show above sand when planted.

3. Place plants, ensuring no soil nears outer edge.

4. Pour quartz sand for lower level, then shake the container to level it.

5. Add hematite sand and shake gently to level.

6. Add clumps of reindeer moss, then scatter the pyrite stones, moving them until you like their placement.

7. Place, and perhaps half-bury, the cube of pyrite in matrix where it can be appreciated.

Care

The 'Black Fancy' begonia and silver squill are easy to grow in part to full sun. Thoroughly water each plant with 1/2 to 3/4 cup of water every 1 to 2 weeks, depending on how quickly they dry out—they prefer soil that dries out between watering. Fertilize monthly with balanced fertilizer diluted to quarter strength. Both plants like to go a bit dry in winter so check surface of soil with fingers before watering.

Tip

Plant the silver squill high, with part of the bulb exposed. To do this, brush away all visible soil from top half of bulbs before planting so that no soil clings to the bulbs above the sand once planted. Silver squill produces flower spikes of tiny greenish-white flowers in spring. 'Black Fancy' begonia produces white flowers in winter.

MAIDENS UNFROCKED

This terrarium design suggests a science experiment in the making—which, in fact, it is. A solid base of creamy quartz sand shows off the spirited, homunculus-like character of the fern roots while the top is animated by a swoop of cinnamon-colored wire vine strands fashioned into a circle.

1 THIN GLASS RECTANGULAR VASE (18 X 8 X 3 INCHES)

4 OLD GLASS BOTTLES: 2 CHINESE APOTHECARY-STYLE BOTTLES AND 2 OLD MEDICINE BOTTLES (ALL VARYING FROM 5 TO 8 INCHES TALL)

4 ROOTED PIECES OF MAIDENHAIR FERN (*Adiantum* species)

6 CUPS PURE QUARTZ SAND

3 SPECKLED ROCKS RESEMBLING BIRDS' EGGS

1 WIRE VINE (*Muhlenbeckia complexa*), STRIPPED OF FOLIAGE

1.   Clean terrarium glass inside and out.

2.   Unpot or dig up from the garden four pieces of maidenhair fern and wash roots in water. Fill the four glass bottles with water and carefully squeeze the fern roots into each bottle. Set aside.

3.   Pour pure quartz sand into the rectangular vase.

4.   Lower the glass bottles onto the sand base—perhaps two face-on and two side-on or in whatever configuration looks best to you.

5.   Haphazardly drop speckled rocks onto sand.

6.   Coil wire vine (stripped of foliage) into a loose circle about the width of the rectangular vase. You can tie it off with itself so that it holds in a rough wreath-shape and drop it into terrarium to rest on the rims of the bottles.

Care

Ferns in water can last for months, even a year, but this is not a permanent home. Enjoy them while the foliage is a nice, rich green and then replace them. You can prolong their vase-life by adding a drop or two of concentrated liquid houseplant food to the water once a month. This terrarium is fairly adaptable—light can range from low to bright, indirect light. Just avoid direct, hot afternoon sun.

Tip

Add varying amounts of water to bottles so that water lines are not the same.

Once ferns begin to yellow, you may wish to plant them in indoor pots (if they are tender in your climate) or, during the growing season, outdoors in a shady part of the garden (if they are cold-hardy in your climate).

RAINFOREST RAINDROP

A glistening, moss- and lichen-filled raindrop suspended in mid-air is a symbol of the life-sustaining precipitation that drenches the lush, verdant rainforest. The combination of black sand, white pebbles, and green moss gives it an elemental feeling, like a time capsule.

1 HANGING TEARDROP VASE (6 INCHES TALL)

JUTE TWINE FOR SUSPENDING TEARDROP

EYE-HOOK OR OTHER CEILING ATTACHMENT

1 CUP HEMATITE SAND

1 SPRIG OLD MAN'S BEARD LICHEN
(*Dolichousnea longissima*)

1 SPRIG FEATHER MOSS (*Ptilium* species)

SMATTERING WHITE PEBBLES

1. Clean terrarium glass inside and out.

2. Attach jute twine to glass and hang before filling to make sure length is correct.

3. Pour hematite sand into teardrop and give it a gentle shake.

4. Coil a sprig of old man's beard lichen into soft ball and poke it through the opening so it sits toward the back.

5. Add a sprig of feather moss and drop white pebbles over some of the bare hematite sand toward the front.

Care

Old man's beard lichen and feather moss both appreciate a bit of indirect light (low or bright is okay). Spritz the living elements a couple of times a week—once a week if in lower light or a cooler location. Or skip the watering and just allow them to dry.

Tip

This terrarium can be suspended and then filled, or filled and then suspended. If you fill it before suspending it, try setting it on a feather pillow or blanket—or in a rubber kitchen bowl to contain excess materials. A dexterous pinkie finger or a piece of bent wire or pipe cleaner are good tools for manipulating pebbles or fluffing moss.

THE TOR

An icy, columnar tower of crystal selenite forms the centerpiece of this terrarium. Named for the Greek moon goddess Selene, selenite has a lovely milky appearance that makes the crystal seem to glow when backlit. Its icy nature is complemented by fire: bring out the light-conducting qualities in the selenite by surrounding the terrarium with small, flickering votive candles.

1 GLASS ALMOND VASE (22 INCHES TALL, 5-INCH OPENING)
6 CUPS PURE QUARTZ SAND
1 LARGE SELENITE SHARD
4 HANDFULS FEATHER MOSS (*Ptilium* species)
14 SMALL SELENITE SHARDS
CHOPSTICKS

1. Clean terrarium glass inside and out.

2. Pour quartz sand into container and gently shake to level.

3. Lower large shard of selenite into the center of the container and twist it down into place.

4. Gently tap container on surface a few times to level sand.

5. Around base of large selenite shard, place small handfuls of the more congested, tightly growing feather moss.

6. Press small selenite shards between the feather moss and the glass, nesting them slightly into the sand. If your hand doesn't fit into the vessel's opening, you can use chopsticks to position small selenite shards.

7. Add the looser, fluffier strands of feather moss toward the top.

Care

In general, feather moss is at its best with medium to bright, indirect natural light. When dried up, feather moss can turn an attractive honey-green shade but to maintain its lovely chartreuse color and fluffiness, mist with a squirt bottle a couple of times a week.

Tip

When you mist moss from above, the water droplets run down the selenite and fog up the glass creating a beautifully atmospheric scene.

LOVE LETTERS FROM VENUS

As seductive and captivating as erotic love itself, this finely formed design represents darkness and light, danger and safety, total transparency with the mystery embodied by the unopened letters. The Venus flytrap, which lures prey with a sweet-smelling nectar and then snaps shut on the hapless insect, brings this terrarium to life while illustrating the inevitability of death.

1 TALL SQUARE GLASS VASE (16 INCHES TALL)

1 STEMMED VOTIVE GLASS (17 INCHES TALL)

1 VENUS FLYTRAP (*Dionaea muscipula* 'Red Dragon')
(2-INCH POT)

1 3/4 CUPS WHITE PEBBLES

1 1/2 CUPS SMALL BLACK ROCKS

2 LARGE, SMOOTH, FLAT WHITE ROCKS

1 PACKET OF HANDMADE PAPER "LETTERS"
BOUND WITH STRING

1. Clean terrarium glass inside and out.

2. If the stemmed votive glass is too long to fit in the tall square vase, you can safely break the stem by wrapping it in a towel or cloth before snapping it.

3. To make inner terrarium: unpot Venus flytrap into stemmed votive glass with all accompanying soil; distribute soil, gently tamping it down to remove air gaps; and cover surface of potting mix with 1/4 cup of white pebbles. Set aside.

4. Add small black rocks to the bottom of the tall square vase. On top of the black rocks, add remaining white pebbles, the large flat white rocks, and the packet of bound "letters."

5. Lower planted stemmed votive glass terrarium into square vase.

Care

Venus flytraps appreciate bright light but should be kept out of direct, hot afternoon sun, which would be intensified in this narrow glass terrarium. A warm, humid environment with constant moisture at the roots is ideal. Water with distilled or rain water. No fertilizer is necessary but if the plants are not trapping any insects, you can deliver meals by dropping insects into the traps. One small bug per week is plenty.

Tip

If you can't find a stemmed votive glass, substitute any stemmed glass that will fit in the opening. You might like to write your own set of love letters or poetry—tie pretty string around it and add to the terrarium.

BARBED BEAUTY

This sweet, sensuous glass orb contains quartz crystals cradled in a bed of tender green moss, while the barbed fish hooks dangling from the base add a literal and figurative element of danger. Although quartz is the second most abundant mineral in the Earth's crust, the clear crystal always seems to have a slight air of mystery. One perfect little piece can be enough to make a small terrarium shine.

1 HANGING BUBBLE VASE (2.5 X 3.5 INCHES)

1/2 CUP WHITE PEBBLES

2 HANDFULS FEATHER MOSS (*Ptilium* species)

1 QUARTZ CLUSTER

4 OLD BARBED FISH HOOKS ON SWIVEL CONNECTOR

2 GLASS CRYSTALS

THREAD FOR ATTACHING HOOKS AND CRYSTALS

JUTE TWINE FOR SUSPENDING VASE

EYE-HOOK OR OTHER CEILING ATTACHMENT

1. Clean terrarium glass inside and out.

2. Pour white pebbles into base and give a gentle shake.

3. Create a small nest with a couple handfuls of feather moss and place it on top of the pebbles.

4. Tuck the cluster of quartz crystals into nest.

5. Fish hooks, glass crystals, and any other small, charming baubles can be attached to the string and tied on.

6. Attach jute twine to bubble vase and hang from a sturdy ceiling hook.

Care

Some kinds of feather moss prefer slightly more or less light or moisture, but in general, feather moss is at its best with indirect natural light. Most feather moss species can be kept healthy—the lovely chartreuse color and fluffiness maintained—by misting with a squirt bottle every few days. When dried up, feather moss can turn an attractive honey-green.

Tip

Don't include the fish hooks if you have children or curious pets in the house. Or hang it well out of reach. You can also replace the sharp hooks with chandelier crystals or other ornaments.

KING OF THE FOREST

This woodland terrarium is populated by fern, lichen, and moss, as well as a variety of natural materials suggesting the gradual decay and renewal that takes place on the forest floor: old shell middens, some scattered rocks, and a set of deer antlers.

1 APOTHECARY JAR (28 INCHES TALL, 8-INCH OPENING)

10 CUPS HEMATITE SAND

4 CUPS BLACK RIVER ROCKS

4 HANDFULS CHARTREUSE FEATHER MOSS (*Ptilium* species)

3 GREEN SEA URCHINS

SMALL DEER ANTLERS

1 MAIDENHAIR FERN (*Adiantum capillus-veneris*) (2- OR 4-INCH POT)

2 HANDFULS OF BEARD LICHEN (*Usnea* species)

1 QUARTZ CLUSTER

1 CUT MEXICAN GEODE

Tip

If antlers are not available, look for bones or keep an eye out for other artfully curved items, whether natural or man-made.

1. Clean terrarium glass inside and out.

2. Pour hematite sand into apothecary jar, turning it on its side and giving it a shake to create a slanted profile.

3. Set black river rocks onto sand all around edges of glass and lay down a bed of chartreuse feather moss on top of it.

4. Slide sea urchins down sides of glass.

5. Settle deer antlers on top of feather moss and tuck potted maidenhair fern in between the antlers.

6. Form a bed with beard lichen for quartz crystal cluster and cut Mexican geode.

7. Finally, bunch the remaining beard lichen around fern pot and fluff it up.

Care

Position terrarium in medium to bright but diffuse light. Once a week, pour approximately 1/2 cup of water directly over center of fern into its pot and mist fern, moss, and lichen a couple of times a week. During spring and summer, fertilize the fern with a quarter-strength solution of balanced liquid fertilizer. The lid is useful for creating a humid environment for the moisture-loving fern but can also trap too much heat within the glass and cause burning. Be sure to keep the terrarium a good distance from a window and out of direct sun, particularly if lid is on. The lid should be removed one day per week to prevent antlers from decaying.

BEACH
TERRARIUMS

DRIFTING REEF

This beautiful arrangement suggests movement and motion, like a slice of ocean life. Intricately webbed, soft lavender sea fan resembles a coral reef backdrop, with gently listing sand mimicking the ocean floor, washed by the ebb and flow of daily tides.

1 RECTANGULAR GLASS TANK (12 X 14 X 5 INCHES)

1 JADE PLANT (*Crassula argentata*) (6-INCH POT)

10 CUPS PURE QUARTZ SAND

2 CUPS WHITE PEBBLES

3 WHITE RIVER ROCKS

1 1/2 CUPS MONTEREY BEACH PEBBLES

1 CHUNK SPIRIT QUARTZ

1 SEA FAN

1. Clean terrarium glass inside and out.

2. Unpot the jade plant and position it to one side of the terrarium (this is the side that will be filled higher with sand).

3. Pour pure quartz sand into terrarium, tilting and shaking it gently to cover base of succulent.

4. Using a small cup or your hands, pour white pebbles around edges of higher side, with some sand showing toward the center.

5. Place the white river rocks near the base of succulent.

6. Pour Monterey beach pebbles on the other side around the edges, up to an inch or so deep, creating a soft downward tilt.

7. Place the chunk of spirit quartz atop the Monterey beach pebbles.

8. Drop the sea fan in back of vignette against glass.

Care

Jade plants prefer bright light; just pull the terrarium away from near window on hot summer days. In winter, keep plant on the dry side, watering every 2 to 3 weeks. In summer, water weekly or whenever soil dries out to the touch by pouring 1/2 to 3/4 cup of water slowly on base of plant. Monthly in spring and summer, add a weak solution of quarter-strength fertilizer to water.

Tip

An evocative element of this design is the resonance of the purple margins on the jade plant against the purple sea fan and the purple tones in the quartz rock. The jade plant will only develop purple margins in bright light—in lower light, leaf margins revert to green. Fortunately, the wide top means heat can escape better, so this terrarium can tolerate brighter light.

ESSENCE OF OCEAN

13

In a reversal of the usual message in a bottle, this apothecary jar aims to contain and distill the ocean rather than keeping it at bay. Like a little ark, this tiny life raft contains a miniature undersea garden of burgeoning plant life juxtaposed with the ancient form of the nautilus, a deep-water ocean mollusk whose spiral-shaped shell embodies the ideal proportions of the golden mean.

1 OLD APOTHECARY JAR (12 X 8 INCHES)

6 CUPS PURE QUARTZ SAND

2 'JADE NECKLACE' CRASSULAS (2-INCH POTS)

1 WOOLLY SENECIO (*Senecio haworthii*) (2- TO 4-INCH POT)

1 CUP WHITE PEBBLES

1 PEARL NAUTILUS SHELL (CENTER CUT)

1 MEDIUM GLASS BUBBLE (3-INCH DIAMETER)

2 SMALL GLASS BUBBLES (2-INCH DIAMETER)

STICK FOR MOVING GLASS BUBBLES

1. Clean terrarium glass inside and out.

2. Pour in two cups of pure quartz sand.

3. Tap the crassulas and the woolly senecio out of their pots and scrape away only topmost surface of soil from their root balls.

4. Position plants as you desire, ensuring that all root balls are an inch or more from the outer edge so soil doesn't show through sand on the sides. Also, position plants so they sit low (they can be lifted as sand is added).

5. Pour the rest of the quartz sand into terrarium at a slight slant; make sure all soil at base of plants is just covered.

6. Add a layer of white pebbles, following the slight slant of the sand.

7. Add the center-cut nautilus shell and 3 glass bubbles. Use a stick to move the glass bubbles around until you like how they are sitting.

Care

Provide bright, indirect light for this terrarium, keeping terrarium well away from the window during hot, sunny days, particularly if jar lid is on. In winter, keep plants on the dry side, watering every 2 to 3 weeks. In summer, water weekly or whenever soil dries out to the touch. Pour 1/4 to 1/2 cup of water slowly directly over root ball of each plant. Apply a solution of quarter-strength fertilizer during spring and summer.

Tip

These succulent plants prefer low humidity so leave the top off the jar after watering to prevent condensation and excessive humidity. Remove top anytime you see condensation.

CELESTIAL BODIES

14

Translucent, starry white crystal on sparkly black sand within a polished glass globe—this design is grounded yet slightly otherworldly. The sheer quantity of glowy crystal, including the extraordinary blue-tinted celestine, irresistibly draw the eye into the center of the glass globe to examine the soft succulent leaves against the angular-faceted crystal pieces.

1 BLOWN-GLASS BUBBLE BOWL (15 X 15 INCHES)

10 CUPS HEMATITE SAND

3 MEDIUM CELESTINE CRYSTAL POINTS

8 LARGE QUARTZ CRYSTAL POINTS

22 SMALL AND MEDIUM QUARTZ CRYSTAL POINTS

1 'CAPE BLANCO' STONECROP (*Sedum spathulifolium* 'Cape Blanco') (4-INCH POT)

SPOON OR STICK

1. Clean terrarium glass inside and out.

2. Pour hematite sand into bowl and give bowl a gentle shake to level sand.

3. Set medium celestine crystal points and large quartz crystal points into sand so they are stable.

4. Scatter small and medium quartz crystal points, shifting it all about until you like how it looks.

5. Pull apart the stonecrop plant. Using a spoon or stick to shift sand, tuck pieces of the stonecrop into sand and cover any exposed soil and roots with sand. Any stonecrop pieces without roots can be placed in sand and will likely root and grow.

Care

Place the terrarium in medium to bright light. Water small sedum plants with a few tablespoons of water about once a week in summer, every 2 weeks in winter, adding quarter-strength balanced fertilizer once a month in spring and summer.

Tip

'Cape Blanco' stonecrop is especially nice with its powdery whitish-blue foliage. It produces acid-yellow flowers in summer and, in full sun, the stems and foliage develop a pinkish tint. If you can't find this particular variety, any small-leaved, grayish stonecrop will do.

A GIRL'S BEST FRIEND

This elegant piece is the Marilyn Monroe of the terrarium world—fluffy, soft, curvy, and spiked with sass—a definite show-stopper and larger-than-life experience. Layers of ermine-white sand, nubbly pebble, smooth river rock, jewel-like sea urchin, raw fluorite rock, and downy clumps of moss are topped with a superstar succulent to create a sparkly, almost edible vision of sensual abundance.

1 CURVY GLASS VASE (32 INCHES TALL)

12 CUPS PURE QUARTZ SAND

6 CUPS WHITE PEBBLES

4 WHITE RIVER ROCKS

4 HANDFULS CREAM REINDEER MOSS

4 HANDFULS CHARTREUSE REINDEER MOSS

1 HANDFUL SMALL MEXICAN RIVER ROCKS, OR OTHER INEXPENSIVE ROCKS

1 *Haworthia venosa* subsp. *tessellata* (2- OR 4-INCH POT)

CHOPSTICKS

3 GREEN SEA URCHINS

5 GREEN RIVER ROCKS

14 RAW FLUORITE ROCKS

1 PIECE OF AMMONITE (FOSSILIZED NAUTILUS SHELL)

Tip

This spectacular piece is large enough to work on the floor but it is equally impressive on a table, where the detail can be seen up close. To water the haworthia, use a small container or turkey baster so you can get your hand down far enough inside the glass.

1. Clean terrarium glass inside and out.

2. Pour pure quartz sand into glass and shake container to settle it.

3. Add white pebbles on a slant.

4. Place white river rocks on one side, with a small bunch of cream reindeer moss above it; add some small Mexican river rocks (or another inexpensive rock) in the center of the terrarium to elevate the plant.

5. Drop the potted haworthia plant in center, followed by more small pinches of cream and chartreuse reindeer moss to conceal the pot. (Chopsticks come in handy to push reindeer moss and other materials into place.)

6. Slide green sea urchins down sides of glass, along with a small pile of green river rocks, the raw fluorite rocks, and the piece of ammonite.

Care

Haworthia venosa subsp. *tessellata* thrives in bright, indirect light or a half to full day of sun; just pull terrarium away from window on hot summer days, as terrarium glass intensifies heat. Water lightly year-round when the soil dries out to the touch. To water, pour 1/2 cup of water slowly at base of plant so water fills inside of pot. Apply a weak solution of quarter-strength fertilizer every other watering during spring and summer.

THE LOST BEACH

This terrarium evokes the sensation of discovering a collection of curious, washed-up debris while walking down a lonesome, foggy beach. A broken, barnacle-encrusted shell, a twisted branch with lichen on it, and a vintage bottle filled with bones meld with rocks and a shapely succulent to create a scene that is perfect in its imperfection.

1 BLOWN-GLASS BUBBLE BOWL (15 X 15 INCHES)

1 TWIG WITH OLD MAN'S BEARD LICHEN
(*Dolichousnea longissima*) ATTACHED

1 CANARY ISLAND AEONIUM (*Aeonium canariense*)
(2- OR 4-INCH POT)

8 CUPS PURE QUARTZ SAND

1 SMALL ANTIQUE BOTTLE WITH SMALL BONES

1 BROKEN SHELL WITH BARNACLES

1 LARGE QUARTZ CRYSTAL POINT

1 WHITE GEODE

2 HANDFULS GREEN RIVER ROCK

1 HANDFUL WHITE PEBBLES

1 HANDFUL OLD MAN'S BEARD LICHEN (*Dolichousnea longissima*)

Tip

This design is at its best using shells found at a beach, not bought. Look for rough shells with barnacles that have an organic, yet balanced, shape. Tiny animal bones can be found in various places, from a dinner plate to one's own garden. They can also be ordered online.

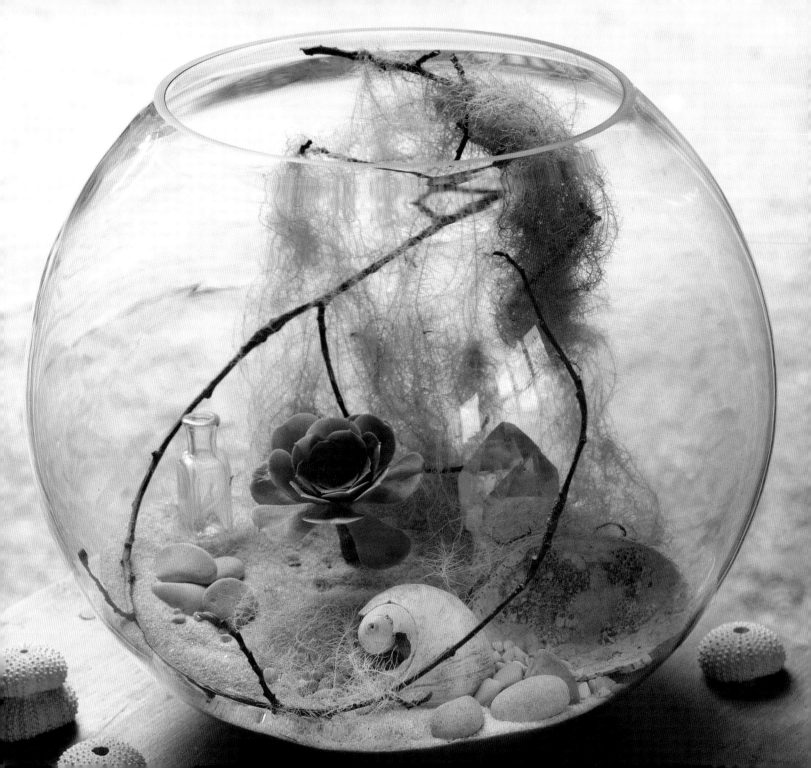

1. Place twig in water overnight, or for at least a couple of hours, until it is pliable.

2. Clean terrarium glass inside and out.

3. Tap the aeonium out of pot and scrape away the topmost surface of soil.

4. Position the aeonium toward center of the bowl and pour pure quartz sand in until all soil at base of plant is covered.

5. Bend the twig into a half-circle and position it in an arc within the terrarium.

6. Place the bone-filled glass bottle, shell, crystal, geode, and green river rocks and move them around until you like how they are sitting. When you're content with it, nest them a bit into the sand for stability.

7. Sprinkle in the white pebbles.

8. Moisten the lichen in water, shake out, and add in puffs behind the aeonium. Finish it off with a few threads of lichen in front.

Care

Bright, indirect light or a half-day of sun is perfect for the succulent. The lichen may decline if light levels are too high but it would still look pretty—or could be refreshed with a new piece of lichen. Mist the lichen a couple of times a week. Slowly pour 1/2 cup of water directly over the roots of the succulent every 1 to 2 weeks (more frequently if positioned in full sun). If in doubt, wait for the succulent foliage to wrinkle slightly before watering.

THE GOLDEN SPIRAL

The nautilus (which means "sailor" in Greek) is an ancient, deep-water ocean mollusk whose spiral-shaped, many-chambered shells are a natural representation of the golden mean, a mathematical principle studied by the ancient Greeks and considered since the Renaissance to be the most perfectly proportioned form in nature.

1 CUT GLASS VASE (8 INCHES TALL)

1 'MANDA'S HYBRID' HAWORTHIA
(*Haworthia* 'Manda's Hybrid') (2- TO 4-INCH POT)

6–8 CUPS HEMATITE SAND

1 CENTER-CUT NAUTILUS SHELL

1/2 CUP SMALL BLACK RIVER ROCKS

3 HERKIMER DIAMONDS

1. Clean terrarium glass inside and out.

2. Add 4 to 5 cups of hematite sand to the base of the container.

3. Tap haworthia out of pot and scrape away only the topmost surface of soil.

4. Position plant toward center of the vase and, holding your hand over the plant to protect foliage, pour in most of the remaining hematite sand until all soil at base of plant is completely covered. The level of the sand should be slightly higher toward the back of the terrarium.

5. Gently shake vase to settle sand and cover any soil that appears with more sand.

6. Place nautilus shell and scatter small black river rocks around base of plant and around two-thirds of the edges of glass, moving them around until you like how they are sitting.

7. Drop the Herkimer diamonds within the arc of the nautilus shell.

Care

'Manda's Hybrid' haworthia enjoys conditions ranging from half or partial sun to bright, diffuse light; just pull terrarium away from window on hot summer days. In winter, keep plant on the dry side, watering every couple of weeks. In summer, water every 1 to 2 weeks (depending on warmth and light levels) by pouring 1/2 cup of water slowly over root ball. Fertilize monthly in spring and summer with quarter-strength balanced fertilizer.

Tip

If the nautilus shell is too long to fit gracefully in the terrarium, just snap it (it breaks easily) and set the piece alongside the rest of the shell in an arc (as in the picture).

SEASIDE CORNUCOPIA

№ 18

Sere as a sandy beach yet brimming with life, this dry cornucopia holds three airplants, living pockets of gray-green beard lichen, and a small bounty of stones including a cluster of quartz, chunks of aragonite, and a scattering of warm orange carnelian agate.

1 BULLET-SHAPED GLASS CANDLEHOLDER
(16 INCHES LONG, 10-INCH OPENING)

5 CUPS PURE QUARTZ SAND

1 'VICTORIANA' AIRPLANT (*Tillandsia* 'Victoriana')

1 BULBOUS AIRPLANT (*Tillandsia bulbosa*)

1 BLUSHING BRIDE (*Tillandsia ionantha*)

1 LARGE QUARTZ CLUSTER

3 CHUNKS ARAGONITE

2 SMALL HANDFULS BEARD LICHEN (*Usnea* species)

6—12 SMALL CARNELIAN AGATE PIECES

1. Clean terrarium glass inside and out.

2. Pour half of the pure quartz sand into glass candleholder and tip onto one side, shaking it to see how much more it can accommodate. Add more sand if needed. Gently shake to level.

3. Settle the airplants in the container with tops toward the open end.

4. Add the quartz cluster and aragonite pieces.

5. Distribute a few small clumps of beard lichen and toss a smattering of carnelian agate on the sand.

Care

Place terrarium where it will receive bright, indirect, or filtered light. Keep it away from direct, hot midday or afternoon sun, as the glass intensifies heat. Every week or two (depending on light levels) remove the airplants from terrarium and submerge in water containing a dilute solution of fertilizer for 1 to 8 hours. Beard lichen can be misted weekly.

Tip

The bullet-shaped glass would also make a lovely horn-of-plenty design, with a profusion of gleanings from the woods and fields (such as plump rosehips, acorns, and flower seedheads) symbolizing fertility, good fortune, and abundance.

FLOWERS FOR MEDUSA

This striking terrarium is built around a dramatic species of airplant with seemingly writhing foliage—Tillandsia caput-medusae—named for the terrifying Greek maiden-goddess with snakes for hair who turned onlookers to stone if they dared to look at her face.

1 GLASS EYE CONTAINER (14 X 16 INCHES, OPENING 2 1/2 INCHES DEEP X 14 INCHES WIDE)

10 CUPS PURE QUARTZ SAND

6 TIGER SHELLS, SMALL AND LARGE

2 LARGE CUT SHELLS

2 LARGE MEDUSA'S HEADS (*Tillandsia caput-medusae*)

3 BLUSHING BRIDES (*Tillandsia ionantha*)

PASTRY BRUSH OR PAINTBRUSH

1. Clean terrarium glass inside and out.

2. Pour quartz sand into vessel, mounding it up two opposite sides slightly.

3. Press the tiger shells softly into the sand. Try positioning the smaller tiger shells closer to the surface and the larger tiger shells about one-third buried.

4. Poke the large cut shells into the sand toward the middle. Nestle the Medusa's heads between the two cut shells with plants' bases sitting on top of the sand.

5. Place the blushing brides near the tiger shells.

Care

Place terrarium where it will receive bright, indirect or filtered light. Avoid direct, hot midday or afternoon sun. Every 1 to 2 weeks (depending on light levels), remove airplants from terrarium and submerge in water containing quarter-strength fertilizer for 1 to 8 hours.

Tip

To create soft sand waves, as in the photograph, use a pastry brush or paintbrush to sweep sand up the sides of the terrarium.

ROCKS IN A RING

Hefty chunks of luminous green fluorite balance the soft frondiness of the mood moss and the tiny, fernlike leaves and delicate white flowers of the "angry bunny," a miniscule carnivorous plant from South Africa.

1 GLASS JAR (5 X 6 INCHES)

2 CUPS SMALL MONTEREY BEACH PEBBLES

1 ANGRY BUNNY PLANT (*Utricularia sandersonii*)

17 RAW FLUORITE STONES

SMALL HANDFUL MOOD MOSS (*Dicranum* species)

1. Clean terrarium glass inside and out.

2. Spread a layer of small pebbles on the bottom of the glass jar and tamp down firmly.

3. Unpot the angry bunny plant and settle into terrarium, spreading out soil mix across the whole surface of terrarium and spreading plant over the surface of soil.

4. Position fluorite stones in a ring around outer edge of the glass.

5. Add a few fluffy pinches of mood moss.

Care

Angry bunny plant, a South African perennial carnivorous plant, appreciates bright, indirect light near a window. Keep soil moist at all times by pouring 1/4 to 1 cup of distilled or rain water over soil regularly and you'll be rewarded with a show of tiny white flowers. Mood moss can be spritzed from time to time, although the humidity of this wet terrarium may keep it green without spritzing.

Tip

In lieu of a sunny window, try a full-spectrum fluorescent light for 18 hours a day. This provides the bright light many carnivorous plants need and will often help them last into a second year indoors. If you can't find fluorite, any chunky mineral that catches your fancy will do.

BASKING IN THE AFTERGLOW

The most pleasing interactions of color and light are sometimes the subtle ones, like the reflection of sunset on ocean waves. The milky pearlescence of the interior of the nautilus shell is the perfect complement to the pinky-lavender-tinted leaves of the succulent ('Afterglow' echeveria) while the reddish stripes on the outside of the nautilus shell play well with the cinnamon-toned Monterey beach pebbles.

1 BRANDY SNIFTER (12 INCHES TALL)

2 CUPS MONTEREY BEACH SAND

2 CUPS MONTEREY BEACH PEBBLES

4 HANDFULS FEATHER MOSS (*Ptilium* species)

1 NAUTILUS SHELL (WHOLE, UNCUT)

2 CUPS WHITE PEBBLES

1 'AFTERGLOW' ECHEVERIA (2- TO 4-INCH POT)

2 HANDFULS NATURAL LICHEN (VARIOUS SPECIES)

Tip

If the plant fits but the pot is too large to slip comfortably in the terrarium, try downsizing the pot: tap it out of the pot, tease some soil out of the roots and tuck snugly in a smaller pot. Note that a 4-inch pot is about as large a pot as will fit in the design. Even then, it's worth measuring the plant's rosette so you know it will fit and look proportionate. If you can't find an 'Afterglow' echeveria, use any variety with pink or lavender leaves.

1. Clean terrarium glass inside and out.

2. Pour Monterey beach sand, followed by Monterey beach pebbles, into base of brandy snifter.

3. Add soft green feather moss in small bunches to form a ring toward the center.

4. Place nautilus shell on its back at the edge of glass so you can gain a glimpse of the pearly interior.

5. Scatter white pebbles around edges.

6. Nestle the 'Afterglow' echeveria (still in pot) within the moss ring, adding natural lichen to conceal the pot.

Care

Indoors, 'Afterglow' echeveria prefers bright light—just pull terrarium away from near window on hot summer days to prevent foliar burn. In winter, keep plant on the dry side, watering every 2 to 3 weeks. In summer, drench plant weekly or whenever soil dries to the touch. To water, pour 1/2 to 3/4 cup of water slowly into pot. Once a month during spring and summer, fertilize with a solution of quarter-strength balanced fertilizer. Spritz feather moss weekly with water to maintain fresh green appearance.

DESERT
TERRARIUMS

ROCK AND ROSE

Looking here much as they would in their native South African habitat, split rock plants are true mimics, having evolved to blend in with neighboring stones to avoid predation by foraging animals. In this terrarium, fragile split rock plants are well camouflaged among river rocks and delicate-looking selenite roses—only to divulge their hiding places in spring when they erupt in showy flower.

1 BLOWN-GLASS BUBBLE BOWL (10 INCHES TALL)

8 CUPS GARNET SAND

1 SPLIT ROCK PLANT
(*Pleiospilos nelii*) (2-INCH POT)

1 'ROYAL FLUSH' SPLIT ROCK PLANT
(*Pleiospilos nelii* 'Royal Flush') (2-INCH POT)

2 CUPS MEXICAN RIVER ROCKS

2 SELENITE ROSES

2 GREEN RIVER ROCKS

5 SMALL RAW PYRITE STONES

Tip

Both the ordinary form of split rock plant and 'Royal Flush' (a selection whose plump leaves are suffused with purple), produce dramatic, 3-inch, pale peach blooms with a white center in summer. Flowers emerge from the cleft at the center of plant. Note that flowering only occurs when plants receive adequate water in the previous months of the growing season.

1. Clean terrarium glass inside and out.

2. Pour half of the garnet sand into terrarium.

3. Tap split rock plants out of pots and position them so they sit low (they can be lifted as sand is added) and scrape top layer of soil away from root balls.

4. Covering plants with your hand so sand does not lodge within crevices, pour remaining garnet sand around plants until no soil shows.

5. Scatter Mexican river rocks over half to two-thirds of the surface area, leaving one or two bare areas with garnet sand showing.

6. Position the selenite roses—perhaps half-burying one of them.

7. Place green river rocks.

8. Drop raw pyrite stones randomly among Mexican river rocks.

Care

Split rock plants do best in bright light with protection from hot afternoon sun in spring and summer, as terrarium glass intensifies heat. Water about 1/4 cup every 1 to 2 weeks in spring through fall, and provide only slight moisture in winter. A weak solution of quarter-strength fertilizer can be added periodically in spring and fall.

CAUDEX VORTEX

What makes this terrarium magical is the majestic beauty of this southern African caudiciform plant, propeller vine (Petopentia natalensis). A caudiciform plant is one with a caudex, or swollen stem, designed to store water in times of drought. With age, the caudex gradually swells, developing a unique character.

1 ROUND PYRAMID GLASS (9 INCHES TALL)
1 PROPELLER VINE (*Petopentia natalensis*)
4 CUPS GARNET SAND
1 CUP MONTEREY BEACH SAND

1. Clean terrarium glass inside and out.

2. While gently holding the propeller vine by the base of the stem in one hand, squeeze sides of pot to loosen with other hand and pull plant from pot. Scrape away topmost layer of soil from root ball.

3. Settle plant's root ball where you want it and pour most of the garnet sand into the container until root ball is covered. Lightly shake the container to settle sand.

4. Add reserved sand to conceal any remaining potting soil and give the container another gentle shake.

5. Dust a layer of yellow Monterey beach sand around edges of terrarium using your hands to direct the sand's fall.

Care

Propeller vine does best in bright filtered light. Avoid strong light as direct sun can burn foliage due to the intensifying effects of the glass terrarium. Every 1 to 2 weeks, pour 1/2 cup of water directly around base of plant. The plant itself is equipped to survive drought so allow it to dry out between watering (though not so much that it wilts). In spring and summer, water with quarter-strength fertilizer every few weeks.

Tip

When selecting your plant subject, look for one whose foliage will not rise above top of terrarium glass. Chances are that a young plant won't have a very well-developed caudex—just be patient! Eventually it will grow and acquire character.

HELLO, ALOE

As tidy and simple as can be, this piece relies on an unusual cut wine glass shape containing a single, perfect aloe plant. This design can be replicated within any kind of stemmed glassware, which almost invites a taste or sip of the beauty.

1 CUT WINE GLASS (12 INCHES TALL)

1 HAWORTHIA-LEAVED ALOE (*Aloe haworthioides*)

1 CUP HEMATITE SAND

1. Clean terrarium glass inside and out.

2. Remove the aloe from its pot, scrape topmost layer of potting soil from root ball, and position plant in the cut wine glass.

3. Holding your hand over the plant to keep sand off the foliage, pour hematite sand around it until root ball is entirely concealed.

4. Gently shake glass to level sand.

Care

Haworthia-leaved aloe prefers part shade to bright filtered light. Maintain the terrarium in a window that receives just dappled morning sun and stringently avoid any direct, particularly hot, afternoon sun. Water every 1 to 2 weeks by pouring 1/2 cup of water around the roots of the plant. Fertilize every few weeks with quarter-strength balanced fertilizer.

Tip

Pick up glass and hold it level when watering so the sand doesn't shift forward.

LAVENDER AND LACE

This sweet, seemingly impromptu vignette speaks in charming volumes: a little bit doting grandma, a little bit sassy young auntie. The soft color of the garnet sand is echoed in the tips of the succulent's leaves and in the reddish-purple sea fan. An ornate silver tray provides a counterpoint to the simplicity of the terrarium itself, while the sea fan looks like a layer of lace.

1 HANGING TEARDROP VASE (9 INCHES TALL)

JUTE TWINE (1-FOOT LENGTH, KNOTTED)

EYE-HOOK OR OTHER CEILING ATTACHMENT
(IF HANGING TEARDROP)

2 CUPS PURE QUARTZ SAND

1 PULIDO'S ECHEVERIA (*Echeveria pulidonis*) (2- TO 4-INCH POT)

2 CUPS GARNET SAND

SILVER AND GOLD HOOP EARRINGS

COYOTE TEETH (FOUND)

OPTIONAL: DRIED REDDISH-PURPLE SEA FAN,
GLASS BOTTLE, OLD SILVER TRAY

Tip

It can be difficult to arrange the hoops and teeth toward the back of the teardrop—just toss them in and enjoy how they land.

1. Clean terrarium glass inside and out.

2. Tie knotted jute twine to glass teardrop. Whether you're making this design to sit on a tray or to suspend from the ceiling, set it up in position before filling it so that your sand and plant are aligned. If set on its side instead of suspended, this teardrop is best placed where it will be stable and won't roll around.

3. Add pure quartz sand and shake to rear of teardrop.

4. Tap echeveria plant out of pot and scrape away topmost surface of soil from root ball.

5. Position echeveria toward center with rosette facing toward the opening and, cupping your hand over it to direct falling sand away from plant, pour garnet sand into terrarium around base of plant and toward the front.

6. Toss silver and gold hoops and coyote teeth behind the echeveria plant.

Care

Pulido's echeveria prefers bright light with some protection from hot, midday summer sun. In summer, water every 1 to 2 weeks or whenever soil dries out to the touch. Pour 1/2 cup of water slowly over center of plant to moisten root ball. Apply a solution of quarter-strength fertilizer occasionally during spring and summer. In winter, keep plant quite dry, watering rarely or only when soil is completely dry, every 3 or more weeks.

THE SHAPE OF TIME

This terrarium beautifully captures the look of the living stone plant in its native, bone-dry, rocky environment. Almost indistinguishable from the river rocks in which it's nestled, this tough natural mimic seems to disappear from sight among the softly rounded, cinnamon-colored stones.

1 CURVY GLASS JAR (5 INCHES TALL)
1 1/2 CUPS PURE QUARTZ SAND
1 LIVING STONE PLANT (*Lithops* species) (2-INCH POT)
FLAT ROCK OR PIECE OF TAPE
1/2 CUP MEXICAN RIVER ROCKS
CHOPSTICKS

1. Clean terrarium glass inside and out.

2. Pour 3/4 cup of the pure quartz sand into terrarium.

3. Tap living stone plant out of pot and carefully scrape the top layer of soil away from root ball.

4. Position the plant so it sits low (it can be lifted as sand is added).

5. Covering plant with flat rock or piece of tape so sand does not lodge within fissure, pour remaining pure quartz sand around plant's base until no soil shows.

6. Drop Mexican river rocks around back and sides of the living stone. Use chopsticks to move the stones around as needed.

Care

Living stones are easy to care for once established, but don't be surprised if you lose a young plant. They do best in bright light with protection from hot afternoon sun in spring and summer. Apply a small amount of water (a few tablespoons) every 2 weeks during the growing season, typically spring until early winter. Then cut back water in winter and just mist occasionally. Quarter-strength fertilizer can be applied in spring and fall.

Living stones are sensitive to cold (temperatures below 40 degrees F) so move terrarium back from window during very cold weather. They are also vulnerable to sunburn, especially when moved quickly from shade to sun, so it's ideal to provide a gradual transition.

Tip

This terrarium is most striking when the living stone plant and rocks are closely matched, as they might be in nature. Living stones are found in shades of cream, gray, brown, and olive green, often with patterns of dark lattice, dots, and lines, which help obscure plants from predators. Search out rocks that help camouflage your living stone plant.

DESERT SOLITUDE

Nested within a simple cut glass vessel, this serene composition of a solitary succulent emerging from apricot sand, glistening amber pebbles, and bleached bone-colored stone evokes the spare, pristine purity of an arid desertscape. The small pieces of carnelian agate sprinkled in front bring out the peachy tones of the sparkly vanadinite.

1 CUT GLASS CONTAINER (8 INCHES TALL)

1 FAIRY WASHBOARD PLANT (*Haworthia limifolia*) (4-INCH POT)

4 CUPS PURE QUARTZ SAND

1 CUP MONTEREY BEACH SAND

2 SELENITE ROSES

1 VANADINITE ON BARITE STONE

1/2 CUP WHITE PEBBLES

1/2 CUP MONTEREY BEACH PEBBLES

1 HANDFUL SMALL CARNELIAN AGATE

Tip

In general, a vessel with a wide opening is an extra-suitable environment for a succulent or cactus because it provides good air circulation and less concentrated heat than a narrow or lidded glass container.

1. Clean terrarium glass inside and out.

2. Add 4 cups of pure quartz sand.

3. Grasp the haworthia by its foliage and squeeze the pot to remove the root ball.

4. Scrape top layer of soil away from the haworthia root ball. Hold succulent with root ball intact so it sits a bit lower than you want it (it can always be lifted after sand is added).

5. Covering the haworthia with your hand so sand does not lodge within leaves, pour Monterey beach sand all around it, covering plant's base with sand until no soil shows.

6. Place the selenite roses and piece of vanadinite on barite.

7. Pour white pebbles around margins of container and add Monterey beach pebbles, blending a bit with the sand.

8. Sprinkle a few carnelian agates in front of the vanadinite on barite.

Care

Haworthias prefer bright light—in full sun, they can develop an attractive reddish cast. To keep green, position where it will receive a half-day of direct light or a full day of bright, indirect light. (Take care to pull away from a blasting, full-sun window in summer, as the concentrated heat in a terrarium can burn haworthia foliage.) Place in full sun in winter. Water haworthia about every 1 to 2 weeks by slowly pouring 1/2 cup of water directly on top of the plant so that water sinks into the root ball. Watch succulents for signs of shriveling or browning tips and increase watering if necessary.

ETERNAL FLAME

A beautiful aged-brass stand in the Art Nouveau–style cradles a curved glass bowl: a dashing setting for a flame-shaped aloe plant. Raw pyrite—from the Greek word meaning "fire"—resembles glowing embers at the base of the aloe torch.

1 GLASS BOWL (6 X 5 INCHES)

1 VINTAGE BRASS STAND (10 INCHES TALL)

5 CUPS MONTEREY BEACH SAND

1 BOWIE'S ALOE (*Aloe bowiea*) (2-INCH POT)

9 SMALL RAW PYRITE STONES

OPTIONAL ALTAR:

3 PIECES OF SOFTWOOD, SUCH AS FIR (DIPTYCH PIECES, 24 X 12 INCHES; BASE 6 INCHES DEEP AND 12 INCHES WIDE)

12 MEDIUM RAW PYRITE STONES FOR BASE OF ALTAR

1. Clean terrarium glass inside and out.

2. Grasp plant by base of foliage and squeeze pot to remove root ball.

3. Scrape top layer of soil away from root ball.

4. Hold plant with root ball intact so it sits low (it can be lifted as sand is added).

5. Covering plant with your hand so sand does not lodge within leaves, pour Monterey beach sand all around plant's base until no soil shows.

6. Situate small raw pyrite stones around the base of the plant.

Care

Bowie's aloe prefers bright light; just pull terrarium away from window on hot summer days, as terrarium glass intensifies heat. In winter, keep plant on the dry side, watering every 2 to 3 weeks. In summer, water plant every 1 to 2 weeks or whenever soil dries out to the touch. Pour 1/2 to 3/4 cup of water slowly over the roots of the plant. Fertilize occasionally with a solution of quarter-strength fertilizer during spring and summer. This glass base is fairly small so beware of overwatering plant, as roots could rot.

Tip

Build a simple altar for this terrarium by cutting the wood backing with a jigsaw in a lancet shape, split down the middle. To achieve the look of a diptych, flip one of the two pieces of wood to show a different grain. The base is made from a separate piece of wood, glued to the back. Attach to the wall with low-profile picture hanging hardware. Leave it rustic, apply gold leaf, or paint it. If you desire, place medium-sized raw pyrite stones around the base of the altar—or leave the space free for something else.

ARC OF DARKNESS

Simple but striking, this design has a dark edge—just a hint of cloak-and-dagger—thanks to the inky underside of the peperomia plant's leaves and the glistening black sand. Against the dark hematite, the quartz sand looks like an unexpected dusting of snow on a volcano.

1 PYRAMID GLASS (11 X 5 INCHES)
1 COSTA RICAN PEPEROMIA (*Peperomia costaricensis*)
5 CUPS HEMATITE SAND
1 CUP PURE QUARTZ SAND

1. Clean terrarium glass inside and out.

2. Gently holding the peperomia plant by the base of the stem in one hand, squeeze sides of pot to loosen with the other hand, and pull plant from pot.

3. Scrape away topmost layer of soil from root ball and settle plant's root ball where you want it.

4. Holding your hand over the plant to protect it, pour most of the hematite sand into container until root ball is covered and gently shake to settle the sand. Add reserved sand to conceal any remaining potting soil and give the container another gentle shake.

5. Dust a layer of quartz sand on top of hematite sand around edges of terrarium using your hands to direct sand's fall and keep sand from landing on plant.

Care

Bright, indirect or dappled, partial sun is ideal for the peperomia. Too little light and the leaves will lose the purple tint and turn green; too much and the leaves will bleach and burn. Peperomia plants also appreciate humidity but need to dry out between watering. Slowly pour approximately 1/2 cup of water directly on base of plant every 1 to 2 weeks, depending on how much light and warmth the plant receives.

Tip

Before watering check soil with fingers to be sure it isn't still damp. If you can't find a Costa Rican peperomia, any other peperomia with small, smooth leaves will do. Peperomias with crinkled leaves will produce a very different look—which you might like!

MÉNAGE À TROIS

Sweet, clean, and simple, this trio of slender bubbly glasses holds a handsomely contrasting collection of tough little succulent plants that vary from one another just enough to command attention. Vive la différence!

3 TAPERED GLASSES (6 AND 7 INCHES TALL)

6 CUPS PURE QUARTZ SAND

1 'TOM THUMB' CRASSULA (2-INCH POT)

1 SILVER SQUILL (*Ledebouria socialis*) (2-INCH POT)

1 RAINBOW BUSH (*Portulacaria afra* 'Variegata') (2-INCH POT)

1/2 CUP WHITE PEBBLES

1 SMALL DECORATIVE BIRD

1. Clean terrarium glass inside and out.

2. Add about 1 cup of pure quartz sand to each container. (Add varying levels of sand to each if making these as a grouping.)

3. Tap the plants out of their pots and scrape away topmost surface of soil. You may need to manipulate the root ball—or snip off edges if root balls are too wide to fit.

4. Place one plant in each glass and pour approximately 1 cup of pure quartz sand around each plant. Be sure to hold your hand over the plants to protect them from the sand. Plant the silver squill high, with part of the bulb exposed. To do this, brush away all visible soil from the top half of bulb before planting so that no soil clings to the bulb above the pebbles.

5. Add white pebbles to the top of each glass.

6. Set the decorative bird into the glass that contains the rainbow bush.

Care

All three plants are adaptable to varying light levels ranging from light shade to bright light. Ideally, position plants where they will receive a half-day of direct light or a full day of bright, indirect light. (Take care to pull away from blasting, full-sun windows in summer.) Water every 1 to 2 weeks by slowly pouring 1/2 cup of water directly over plant so that water sinks into the root ball. Watch for signs of shriveling or browning tips and increase watering if necessary. Apply a balanced quarter-strength fertilizer monthly during spring and summer.

Tip

The narrow bases and slender profiles of these glasses makes them perfect additions to a windowsill—particularly one you look at closely every day, such as in front of the kitchen sink!

TEST TUBE BABIES

Two clear glass test tubes—perfect for incubating live organisms—offer two small succulents a better life through science. Fill them in with sedimentary layers of materials from the Earth's crust and watch the plants grow.

2 TEST TUBES (8 X 1 1/2 INCHES)

1 CUP CRUSHED LAVA ROCK

1/4 CUP MONTEREY BEACH PEBBLES

1 HANDFUL SMALL BLACK RIVER ROCKS

2 SPRIGS CREAM REINDEER MOSS

1 SUNRISE PLANT (*Anacampseros telephiastrum* 'Variegata') (2- TO 4-INCH POT, WITH POTTING MIX)

1 CUP MONTEREY BEACH SAND

1 JADE PLANT (*Crassula ovata*) IN BLOOM (2- TO 4-INCH POT, WITH POTTING MIX)

JUTE TWINE FOR SUSPENDING TEST TUBES

EYE-HOOK OR OTHER CEILING ATTACHMENT

1. Clean terrarium glass inside and out.

2. Add the following materials to the first test tube, tamping down firmly after each addition: crushed lava rock, a thin layer of Monterey beach pebbles, a handful of small black river rocks, and a sprig of cream reindeer moss. Then, unpot the sunrise plant, scraping away the topmost surface of soil, and add the plant with potting mix. Finish by sprinkling a layer of Monterey beach pebbles over the top surface.

3. For the second test tube, add most of the Monterey beach sand and then a sprig of cream reindeer moss. Tamp down after each addition. Unpot the jade plant, scraping away the topmost surface of soil, and add the plant with potting mix. Finish by sprinkling a layer of Monterey beach sand on top.

4. Wrap jute twine a few times underneath test tube rims. Knot to secure it and suspend from secure eye-hooks.

Care

The sunrise plant and jade plant both prefer bright light—just protect terrarium from direct sun during the hottest summer months. Water every 1 to 2 weeks in summer; every 2 to 3 weeks in winter. Fertilize occasionally in spring and summer with quarter-strength balanced fertilizer.

Tip

It is important to tamp the materials after each addition so that the layers are crisp and tightly packed. You can use the blunt end of a wood stake or anything you have around with a flat end.

It's fine—and often desirable—if the tubes don't hang exactly level.

TERRESTRIAL ORB

Clean, simple, and totally self-contained—as perfect a sight as a star in the night sky. Baseball plant (Euphorbia obesa) often exhibits beautiful patterning and ribbing which makes it a worthy subject of contemplation. Luckily, every inch of this divine succulent can be admired up close through the chunky, clear, glass square.

1 SHORT PYRAMID GLASS (5 INCHES TALL)

5 CUPS MONTEREY BEACH SAND

1 BASEBALL PLANT (*Euphorbia obesa*) (2- OR 4-INCH POT)

PASTRY BRUSH OR PAINTBRUSH

3 CUPS PURE QUARTZ SAND

1. Clean terrarium glass inside and out.

2. Pour 1 cup of Monterey beach sand into terrarium, forming a hill toward the center.

3. Tap the baseball plant out of pot, scrape away topmost surface of soil, and position plant toward center on "hill."

4. Cupping your hand over it to protect it from the sand, pour 3 more cups of Monterey beach sand into the terrarium around plant.

5. Use a brush to push sand up a bit toward center, following the arc of the glass container's base.

6. Add 1 cup of pure quartz sand—pour around the edges of the glass first, then move in to the center once you have covered the edges.

7. With the remaining Monterey beach sand, create another layer, pouring it first around the edges.

8. Use the remaining pure quartz sand to fill in around the plant.

9. Contour the top layer with the brush.

Care

Baseball plant thrives in bright, indirect light, or a half to full day of sun; just pull terrarium away from window on hot summer days, as terrarium glass intensifies heat. In winter, keep plant on the dry side, watering every 2 to 3 weeks. In summer, water plant every 1 to 2 weeks or whenever soil dries out to the touch. To water, pour 1/2 cup of water slowly on top of plant so water drips down sides onto roots. Apply a weak solution of quarter-strength fertilizer every other watering during spring and summer.

Euphorbias emit a white sap that can be toxic or poisonous. After handling euphorbias, always wash your hands thoroughly and avoid touching your eyes.

Tip

Baseball plant can feel top-heavy when unpotting, as if the top could separate from the delicate roots. Hold plant securely by top so the roots aren't damaged while transplanting and be sure plant sits securely in sand and doesn't wiggle once planted.

SUSPENDED HEARTS

A tangle of hearts resting on a bed of crystalline quartz sand—a tiny tempest in a teardrop. As the vine grows, the petite, heart-shaped leaves spill luxuriantly out of the teardrop; clip them or let them flow forth.

1 HANGING TEARDROP VASE (9 INCHES TALL)
JUTE TWINE FOR SUSPENDING TEARDROP
EYE-HOOK OR OTHER CEILING ATTACHMENT
3 CUPS PURE QUARTZ SAND
1 STRING OF HEARTS VINE (*Ceropegia woodii*) (2- OR 4-INCH POT)

1. Clean terrarium glass inside and out.

2. Attach jute twine to glass and hang before filling to make sure length is correct.

3. Tilt the teardrop backward and pour in about 1 cup of pure quartz sand.

4. Tap the string of hearts vine out of pot and scrape top layer of soil away from root ball.

5. Swirl long strands of vine into an artful tangle (try rolling it in a loose circle, with a strand or two teased out so it can hang from front opening).

6. Position the tangled vine toward the center of the terrarium and hold it up in one cupped palm while pouring in most of the remaining pure quartz sand with your other hand until base of plant is completely covered.

7. Tilt teardrop upright again and give a little shake to level sand. Use reserved quartz sand to cover the plant's base if any soil is visible.

Care

String of hearts vine prefers bright to partial light, with some protection from hot, midday summer sun. In summer, water every 1 to 2 weeks or whenever soil dries out to the touch. Pour 1/2 cup of water slowly over center of plant (root ball). Apply a solution of quarter-strength fertilizer occasionally during spring and summer. In winter, keep plant on the dry side, watering every 2 to 3 weeks or when soil is completely dry. The plant resents overwatering so be sure roots dry out between watering.

Tip

String of hearts vine develops a caudex (swollen, woody stem) over time. Under optimal conditions, this succulent vine from South Africa, Swaziland, and Zimbabwe will produce upturned, tubular, lavender to purple flowers with maroon stamens in summer and fall, particularly when roots are slightly crowded.

GREEN SILKWORMS

This terrarium's considerable charm lies in the contrast between the dynamic, lively, larval form of the crassula plant and the neatly arranged, static formality of the carefully—even meticulously—patterned sand below.

1 TALL GLASS PYRAMID (12 INCHES TALL)

6 CUPS PURE QUARTZ SAND

1 CUP GARNET SAND

1 JADE NECKLACE PLANT (*Crassula rupestris* subsp. *marnieriana*) (2-INCH POT)

1. Clean terrarium glass inside and out.

2. Pour 4 cups of pure quartz sand into the terrarium.

3. Add a thin layer of garnet sand (1/4 cup), ensuring each side of the glass has a thin line of sand (although a little imperfection can be lovely too).

4. Continue layering 1/4 cup of pure quartz sand and 1/4 cup of garnet sand until there are three lines of garnet sand.

5. Grasp plant by base of foliage and squeeze pot to remove root ball.

6. Scrape top layer of soil away from root ball. Hold plant with root ball intact so it sits a bit lower than you want it (it can always be lifted as sand is added).

7. Covering plant with your hand so sand does not lodge within leaves, pour pure quartz sand all around plant's base until no soil shows.

8. Scatter the remaining garnet sand on the top surface.

Care

Jade necklace plant needs bright light but make sure to protect it from the hottest afternoon sun, as the ultra narrow terrarium glass intensifies heat. In winter, keep plant a little on the dry side, watering every 2 to 3 weeks. In summer, water weekly or whenever soil dries out to the touch. Pour 1/2 cup of water slowly onto plant. Water with a solution of quarter-strength fertilizer during spring and summer.

Tip

Crassula root balls can fall apart easily, so grasp the plant's stems and hold them together until you have secured it in the sand.

If the plant gets too dry a leaf may randomly die out along the stem. If this happens, you can cut the stem below the dried leaf and it will branch from that point.

CLAIR DE LUNE

Fine quartz sand layered with bands of nobbly white pebbles forms a solid base for a topdressing of larger cream and green river rocks and a striking, lustrous crystal point. The smooth, worn stones intensify the dramatic, undulating margins of the plant's leaves. The pale, subtle colors seem almost to be bathed in moonlight.

1 GLASS CYLINDER (12 X 8 INCHES)

6 CUPS PURE QUARTZ SAND

PASTRY BRUSH OR PAINTBRUSH

8 CUPS WHITE PEBBLES

1 HANDFUL NATURAL LICHEN

1 SILVER CROWN PLANT (*Cotyledon undulata*)
(2- OR 4-INCH POT)

1 LARGE QUARTZ CRYSTAL POINT

2 HANDFULS GREEN RIVER ROCKS

2 HANDFULS WHITE RIVER ROCKS

4 SMALL AND MEDIUM QUARTZ POINTS

1 SMALL CITRINE POINT

Tip

To prevent sand sifting down, tamp top layer of white pebbles firmly before adding lichen and plant—then gently add layer of sand. And avoid shaking or moving this terrarium, as sand tends to shift over time.

1. Clean terrarium glass inside and out.

2. Add 3 cups of pure quartz sand to base of container and brush sand up in a curve as high as possible on just one side.

3. To the low side, add 4 cups of white pebbles, tamping them down to settle. Pour 1 cup of pure quartz sand in a layer over white pebbles, followed by the rest of the white pebbles, still on the low side.

4. Make a small bed of lichen, leaving the center open.

5. Tap silver crown plant out of pot, nestle into lichen, and pour the remaining 2 cups of pure quartz sand around it to "plant" it.

6. Place quartz crystal, point facing up, near the plant.

7. Loosely pile green river rocks and white river rocks around edges of cylinder.

8. Position quartz and citrine points.

Care

Silver crown plant thrives in bright, indirect light or a half to full day of sun; just pull terrarium away from window on hot summer days, as terrarium glass intensifies heat. In winter, keep plant on the dry side, watering every 2 to 3 weeks. In summer, water plant every 1 to 2 weeks or whenever soil dries out to the touch. To water, pour 1/2 cup of water slowly on base of plant so water reaches roots. Apply a weak solution of quarter-strength fertilizer every other watering during spring and summer.

UNDER AFRICAN SKIES

This large golden globe suffuses the sand and living stone plants with the warm amber glow of a shimmering hot South African afternoon. The fact that the terrarium contains water adds an intriguing layer of complexity. If living stones could dream, they would surely dream of water—so tantalizingly close yet impossible to reach.

1 BLOWN-GLASS BUBBLE BOWL (15 X 15 INCHES)

12 CUPS MONTEREY BEACH SAND

7 LIVING STONE PLANTS (*Lithops* species)

1 LARGE COOPER'S HAWORTHIA PLANT
(*Haworthia cooperi* var. *pilifera*)

PASTRY BRUSH OR SMALL PAINTBRUSH

VINTAGE AMBER VASE ON PEDESTAL

2 SMALL PIECES OF BRACKET FUNGUS

1 HANDFUL MONTEREY BEACH PEBBLES

1 HANDFUL WHITE PEBBLES

A FEW ORNAMENTAL GRASS FLOWER STALKS IN VASE
(HERE, *Pennisetum orientale* 'Karley Rose' AND AN
UNIDENTIFIED ROADSIDE WEED)

Tip

Living stone roots are fragile so be very careful when you scrape the soil away from the root ball.

When planting this terrarium, you might have better luck with the haworthia if you decide which will be the window-side (sunny) and position the haworthia plants on the shady side of the bracket fungi or any outcroppings you might add. Alternatively, you might try replacing the haworthia with a petite, yet more sun-tolerant succulent with a similar look.

1. Clean terrarium glass inside and out.

2. Pour 6 cups of Monterey beach sand into terrarium, creating a slightly higher level in back.

3. Determine where vase will sit and keep a suitable amount of space clear for it.

4. Tap living stone plants out of pots and carefully scrape top layer of soil away from root balls.

5. Unpot the haworthia and separate it into individual lobes so you have 7 small plants, each with a little soil attached.

6. Position plants on sand base so they sit low (they can be lifted as sand is added) and, keeping sand out of the living stone plants' crevices, pour remaining Monterey beach sand around plants' bases until no soil shows.

7. Use a pastry brush or small paintbrush to contour sand and, while you're at it, brush any sand out of plants' foliage. Gently lift any plants that are planted too deeply (you want soil level to be just below sand).

8. Settle vase in terrarium, adjusting surrounding plants slightly if needed.

9. Place the bracket fungi and scatter handfuls of Monterey beach pebbles and white Asian pebbles.

10. Pour water into vase and arrange grass flower stalks in vase.

Care

Living stones are easy to care for once established, but don't be surprised if you lose a young plant. They do best in bright light with protection from hot afternoon sun in spring and summer. Apply a small amount of water (a few tablespoons) every 2 weeks during the growing season, typically spring until early winter. Then cut back water in winter and just mist occasionally. Quarter-strength fertilizer can be applied in spring and fall.

Living stones are sensitive to cold (temperatures below 40 degrees F) so move terrarium back from window during very cold weather. They are also vulnerable to sunburn, especially when moved quickly from shade to sun, so it's ideal to provide a gradual transition.

CRESCENT MOON

The epitome of simplicity, this exquisitely formed echeveria with garnet-suffused leaf undersides sits atop a bed of garnet sand, like an impeccable porcelain rose. This little vessel of beauty is about as visually perfect as a terrarium can be.

1 GLASS CONTAINER (8 X 8 INCHES)
1 'LOLA' ECHEVERIA (4-INCH POT)
5 CUPS GARNET SAND
1 CUP PURE QUARTZ SAND

1. Clean terrarium glass inside and out.

2. To unpot the echeveria, gently squeeze sides of pot to loosen while pulling plant from pot with other hand.

3. Scrape away topmost layer of soil from root ball.

4. Settle plant's root ball where you want it and pour most of the garnet sand into container until root ball is covered. Gently shake the container to settle sand.

5. Add reserved garnet sand to conceal any remaining potting soil and give it another gentle shake.

6. Dust a layer of pure quartz sand around edges of terrarium using your hands to direct sand's fall.

Care

Indoors, echeverias prefer bright light; just pull terrarium away from window on hot summer days. In winter, keep plant on the dry side to avoid rot, watering lightly every 2 to 3 weeks. In summer, drench plant weekly (or whenever soil dries out to the touch) by slowly pouring 1/2 cup of water onto the roots of the plant. Use a weak solution of quarter-strength fertilizer every other week during spring and summer.

Tip

This design depends on a perfect plant! Groom plant carefully, pulling out any damaged leaves—or leaving them if they look interestingly withered. Just be careful about poking the fleshy foliage with anything sharp, as such damage shows up permanently. Also, excessive handling leaves finger prints when you rub the powdery coating off the surface of the foliage.

DOS PUEBLOS

This design conjures up the lost world of meso-American indigenous civilization—a village of tiny cliff dwellings, surrounded by gravel and with enormous aloes (actually, teeny-weeny echeveria plants, but who's telling?) dotting the landscape.

2 SQUARE GLASS VASES WITH RIMS
(6 INCHES AND 5 INCHES TALL)

2 DWARF ECHEVERIAS (*Echeveria bella* f. *bella*)

9 CUPS MONTEREY BEACH SAND

2 HAND-CARVED VINE BARK MEXICAN HOUSES
(ONE SMALL, ONE LARGE)

5 SMALL PIECES DRIFTWOOD

1 SMALL HANDFUL MONTEREY BEACH PEBBLES

1/4 CUP PURE QUARTZ SAND

1. Clean terrarium glass inside and out.

2. Grasp echeveria plants by base of foliage, squeeze pot to remove root balls, and scrape top layer of soil away from root balls.

3. In the larger glass vase, place plants with root balls intact so they sit low (they can be lifted as sand is added), positioning them to one side so that there will be room for the smaller house. Cover plants with your hand (so sand does not lodge within leaves) and pour 6 cups of Monterey beach sand all around them until no soil shows. Position a large chunk of driftwood to one side at the back, with the small Mexican house in a cozy spot toward the other side at the back. Lay Monterey beach pebbles for a path.

4. In the smaller vase, pour 3 cups of Monterey beach sand. Set remaining pieces of driftwood at back of terrarium and place larger house in front of it, leaving some room in the front for an arc of dusted pure quartz sand.

Care

Provide bright light for the echeverias, remembering to pull terrarium away from the window on hot summer days, as terrarium glass intensifies heat. In winter, keep plants on the dry side, watering every 2 to 3 weeks. In summer, water weekly or whenever soil dries out to the touch. Pour 1/2 to 3/4 cup of water slowly over center of plants. Apply a solution of quarter-strength fertilizer occasionally during spring and summer.

Tip

It's especially fun to build these terrariums as a pair, creating a village-like feeling. If you are particularly ambitious, you can add to the grouping—just increase the amount of materials proportionally. If Mexican bark houses are not available, try little toy houses made out of other materials. Tiny, handmade houses are interesting to find in crafts markets, both local and foreign.

FANTASY
TERRARIUMS

BIRD BY BIRD

Fun, playful, a little bit daffy—and yet exquisite in its dollhouse-like proportions—this miniscule assemblage resembles a tiny songbird fairyland. Each of the three spice jars and the moss "island" presents a different blend of materials and an opportunity for creative expression. Perfect child's play for any age.

3 SPICE JARS WITHOUT LIDS (3 INCHES TALL)

1 HANDFUL MOOD MOSS (*Dicranum* species)

2 SMALL BIRDS AFFIXED TO WIRE (1 1/2 INCHES TALL)

2 SILK BRANCHES WITH FLOWER BUDS

10 SMALL POLISHED BLACK ROCKS

1/2 HANDFUL NATURAL LICHEN (*Cladonia rangiferina*)

1/2 HANDFUL CHARTREUSE REINDEER MOSS

5 VERY SMALL SILK FLOWERS

1 SAGRA BEETLE

1 SPRIG OLD MAN'S BEARD LICHEN (*Dolichousnea longissima*)

OPTIONAL: THICK SLAB OF WEATHERED, OLD WOOD (ABOUT 2 X 18 X 6 INCHES) AND A MAPLE SAMARA

1. Clean terrarium glass inside and out.

2. Make the moss island by cutting a dry chunk of mood moss into a circle (about 1/2 handful). Poke a little bird on a wire and two small faux branches with flower buds into the moss. Add several small black polished rocks on top.

3. Layer 1/2 handful of mood moss into one jar, placing dead sagra beetle in front center.

4. Layer 1/2 handful of lichen into the next jar, placing silk flowers around front.

5. In the third jar, add 1/2 handful of chartreuse reindeer moss and the sprig of old man's beard lichen. Place decorative bird and additional polished black rocks on top.

6. Place moss island, jars, and maple samara on a slab of weathered wood—or not, as you like.

Care

No care required unless you want to keep the mood moss a fresh green color. If so, just mist it once a week. If not, the moss will turn a lovely honey-green as it dries.

Tip

Position these tiny vignettes so you can view them from the front and sides nicely. These are wonderfully cute and accessible terrariums for children to make, with grown-up help.

FROM GRANDMA'S JEWEL BOX

This colorful, elegant presentation sets grandma's favorite old piece of jewelry in a favorable light. A little old-fashioned, a little ornate, this special design includes soft, time-worn river rock, a faded silk rose, the magical sparkle of crystal inside the crusty façade of a geode, and a tough succulent plant in the middle, standing proud.

1 BULLET CONTAINER (23.5 INCHES TALL)

6 CUPS MONTEREY BEACH PEBBLES

2 LARGE HANDFULS FEATHER MOSS (*Ptilium* species)

3 QUARTZ POINTS

1 STRING OF BUTTONS PLANT (*Crassula perforata*)
(6-INCH PLANT)

1 HANDFUL GREEN RIVER ROCKS

1 SILK FLOWER

1 SMALL FEATHER

1 OLD-FASHIONED FAUX-DIAMOND BROOCH

1 MEXICAN GEODE

2 HANDFULS CHARTREUSE REINDEER MOSS

1 SPRIG CREAM REINDEER MOSS

1. Clean terrarium glass inside and out.

2. Pour 6 cups of Monterey beach pebbles into the bottom of the container.

3. Add handfuls of feather moss around edges of container, and layer quartz points against glass.

4. Set the potted string of buttons plant on pebbles and place green river rocks around base. Drop in silk flower, feather, and brooch and set Mexican geode with crystalline interior facing "front."

5. Add puffs of chartreuse and cream reindeer moss to conceal pot.

Care

String of buttons plant thrives in bright, indirect light or a half day of sun; just pull terrarium away from window on hot summer days, as terrarium glass intensifies heat. In winter, keep plant on the dry side, watering every 2 to 3 weeks. In summer, water plant every 1 to 2 weeks or whenever soil dries out to the touch. To water, pour 1/2 cup of water slowly on base of plant so water reaches roots. Apply a weak solution of quarter-strength fertilizer every other watering during spring and summer.

Tip

This is a great terrarium in which to use that lovely piece of broken or costume jewelry that you love but will never wear. It can be as subtle or as gaudy as you like.

TINY BUBBLES

Suspended like dewdrops, these tiny reflective vases invite closer inspection thanks to the diversity of intriguingly "primitive" natural materials—bones, stones, moss, and lichen—and the sparkle of some carnelian agates. Unlike the fleeting lifespan of dewdrops, this no-maintenance arrangement is frozen in time.

6 MINI-DECO VASES (3 INCHES HIGH)

6 STRANDS OF GOLD THREAD (VARYING LENGTHS)

EYE-HOOK OR OTHER CEILING ATTACHMENT

3 SPRIGS CHARTREUSE REINDEER MOSS

2 SPRIGS CREAM REINDEER MOSS

8 SMALL BONES

1/2 HANDFUL WHITE PEBBLES

1/4 HANDFUL MONTEREY BEACH PEBBLES

25 SMALL CARNELIAN AGATE STONES

1 SPRIG OLD MAN'S BEARD LICHEN (*Dolichousnea longissima*)

1. Clean terrarium glass inside and out.

2. Knot gold thread around the neck of each vase and suspend them at varying heights from a sturdy ceiling hook.

3. To each vase, add a mix of raw materials that pleases you. From top to bottom, the vases in the photograph include: a sprig of chartreuse reindeer moss with some Monterey beach pebbles; a clump of cream reindeer moss plus a few small carnelian agate stones; bones; a sprig each of cream and chartreuse reindeer moss and a sprig of old man's beard lichen; a sprig of chartreuse reindeer moss and a bunch of small carnelian agate stones; a sprig each of cream and chartreuse reindeer moss with some white pebbles.

Care

This terrarium is great for any environment, as it requires no light, water, or care. If you wish, you can spritz the clump of old man's beard lichen from time to time. But even if you don't, it will still look beautiful.

Tip

Hang against a white wall or near a window or light to illuminate the contents.

OMNIUM GATHERUM

The textures nestled within these French canning jars are as delicately paired as the elements of a multi-course Parisian meal: crunchy and soft, airy and earthy, matte and glisteny, smooth and rough, and verdant and flowery. Deliciously sensual but definitely non-fattening.

3 "LE PARFAIT" FRENCH CANNING JARS (10 AND 5 INCHES TALL)

2 CUPS BLACK RIVER ROCKS

4 HANDFULS FEATHER MOSS (*Ptilium* species)

3 1/2 HANDFULS CREAM REINDEER MOSS

2 SILK FLOWERS

3 CUPS MONTEREY BEACH PEBBLES

1 HANDFUL POLISHED BLACK RIVER ROCK

3 HANDFULS CHARTREUSE REINDEER MOSS

A PRETTY SHELL OF YOUR CHOICE

1 HANDFUL GREEN RIVER ROCKS

2 GLASS BUBBLES (SMALL AND LARGE)

1. Clean terrarium glass inside and out.

2. For the jar on the left: place 2 cups of black river rocks on the bottom of jar; add 2 handfuls of feather moss and 1/2 handful each of cream and chartreuse reindeer mosses; slide a silk flower down the side of the glass.

3. For the jar in the middle: pour 1 cup of Monterey beach pebbles in the jar; place a handful of polished black river rocks; add 1 handful each of cream and chartreuse reindeer mosses; nestle shell in the moss against the glass.

4. For the jar on the far right: pour 2 cups of Monterey beach pebbles into the bottom of jar; set in a few green river rocks on their edges; tear remaining handfuls of reindeer mosses and feather moss into smaller pieces and build up a little moss "wall" along one side of the jar; place glass bubbles and silk flower.

Care

These terrariums require the absolute bare minimum of care. If you wish to retain the rich green color of the feather moss, you can spritz it from time to time. Otherwise, it will dry to an attractive honey-green.

Tip

Bubbles look loveliest suspended higher up the side of the glass, and together. Add the flowers toward the top if you want to balance up the heft of the base. Choose both tightly congested and looser pieces of reindeer moss for some diversity.

THE OLD VICTROLA

43

Layers of dark, glistening sand, light and creamy tiny shells, and fluffy bright green mood moss provide textural tiers of bedding for a funny little trinket. The trinket can be anything, from a child's toy to a beloved, pocket-sized heirloom. Sometimes just setting an object in a place of honor is all that's needed to really "see" it.

1 GLASS SCIENCE JAR (9 INCHES TALL)

6 CUPS HEMATITE SAND

1 1/2 CUPS TINY MIXED SHELLS

2 HANDFULS MOOD MOSS (*Dicranum* species)

1 OLD TOY PHONOGRAPH (3 INCHES TALL) OR ANY OTHER TRINKET

1 BUDDED SILK FLOWER BRANCH

1. Clean terrarium glass inside and out.

2. Pour in hematite sand, mounding it up a bit in the center.

3. Pour shells around edges against glass.

4. Add a chunk of well-spritzed mood moss in center, fluffy side up.

5. Set trinket on moss bed and add silk flower branch.

Care

No care required unless you want to keep moss a fresh green color. If so, spritz moss regularly, perhaps weekly, and provide at least a bit of natural light. If the moss isn't watered or given light, it will turn a lovely honey-green as it dries.

Tip

You can use a real branch if you like—for instance, a dried rose branch studded with thorns and hips, or a fresh branch from a flowering quince, dogwood or Japanese maple. To help the branch stay fresh longer try nestling a tiny florist's vial of water (used for corsages) into the moss and tuck one end of the branch into the concealed vial.

TRILOGY

44

This raindrop-like chain of glass bubbles contains a carefully curated collation of natural, elemental materials: fiery carnelian agate, meandering airplants, watery crystal calcite, and earthy brown, folded paper art.

3 HANGING BUBBLE VASES (EACH 2.5 X 3.5 INCHES)

JUTE TWINE FOR SUSPENDING VASES

EYE-HOOK OR OTHER CEILING ATTACHMENT

1 1/2 CUPS PURE QUARTZ SAND

4 CLEAR CALCITE CRYSTALS

3 BULBOUS AIRPLANTS (*Tillandsia bulbosa*)

3 HANDMADE PAPER DECORATIONS (OLD BOOKS)

1 PRECIOUS WENTLETRAP SHELL

2 SMALL, DOWNY DOVE FEATHERS

SMALL SPOON

1 HANDFUL CARNELIAN AGATE PEBBLES

1 PIECE OF THIN, COLORED THREAD (12 INCHES LONG)

1. Clean terrarium glass inside and out.

2. Attach the jute twine to the topmost bubble vase, looping and knotting it through a stable eye-hook or other ceiling attachment so it hangs straight. Next, tie twine to the second bubble vase, loop it through the hook at the bottom of the first and knot it. Repeat with the third bubble vase.

3. Add quartz sand to each bubble vase and gently shake all of them, starting with the topmost bubble.

4. Distribute materials among the three vases: calcite crystals, airplants, paper decorations, wentletrap shell, and downy dove feathers. Using a small spoon, scatter carnelian agate pebbles here and there.

5. Tie one of the paper decorations to a strand of thin, colored thread from the bottom bubble.

Care

Hang this trio of bubble vases where it will receive bright or filtered light but will be protected from hot, midday sun. Every week or two, depending on brightness of location, remove all three airplants and soak in water diluted with quarter-strength fertilizer for 1 to 8 hours.

Tip

If you can't find a precious wentletrap, there are many other similar varieties. Or just use a favorite shell you picked up on the beach.

45

ICE QUEEN

This richly textured, tapestry-like composition includes wood, stone, mineral, fungus, moss, lichen, and a little amalgam of succulent plants, crowned with a regal aloe. It's a little bit desert, a little bit beach, a little bit forest, and a big bit fantasy.

1 BLOWN-GLASS BUBBLE BOWL (20 X 20 INCHES)

12 CUPS BLACK RIVER ROCKS

6 BIG HANDFULS FEATHER MOSS
(*Ptilium crista-castrensis*)

8 LARGE QUARTZ CRYSTAL POINTS

1 DELTA-SHAPED ALOE
(*Aloe deltoideodonta* var. *candicans*) (4- TO 6-INCH POT)

2 'FRED IVES' GRAPTOVERIAS
(*Graptoveria* 'Fred Ives') (2- TO 4-INCH POTS)

2 DESERT SURPRISE PLANTS
(*Kalanchoe humilis*) (2- TO 4-INCH POTS)

3—4 SMALL PIECES OF DRIFTWOOD

6 PIECES BRACKET FUNGUS
(ALSO KNOWN AS "CONKS")
RANGING IN SIZE FROM LARGE TO SMALL

1 HANDFUL CHARTREUSE REINDEER MOSS

Tip

Balancing the "conks" so they stay put in the moss can be a challenge. Try stabilizing them with extra little bunches of moss. The conks can be gathered in private woodland (with permission!) from pieces of rotting wood.

An extra-small-sized spritzer bottle may be needed to reach all the feather moss inside the terrarium.

1. Clean terrarium glass inside and out.

2. Set a layer of polished black river rocks in base.

3. Form a bed of feather moss upon which to set potted succulents.

4. Set in crystals against edges of glass bowl.

5. Place the aloe in the center of the moss bed, flanked by the graptoverias and desert surprise plants. Tuck more feather moss around pots to completely cover pot rims and bases of plants if necessary.

6. Place driftwood pieces, bracket fungi, and small pieces of chartreuse reindeer moss.

Care

Provide bright light for this terrarium, particularly for the graptoverias and desert surprise plants, remembering to pull terrarium away from the window on hot summer days, as terrarium glass intensifies heat. In winter, keep plants on the dry side, watering every 2 to 3 weeks. In summer, water every 1 to 2 weeks or whenever soil dries out to the touch. Pour 1/2 cup of water slowly into smaller pots; the aloe may require slightly more water (3/4 cup) than the other plants. Water with a solution of quarter-strength fertilizer during spring and summer. Since this terrarium should be in a bright, sunny spot, feather moss should be misted several times a week. The bracket fungi require no special care or water.

FEATHER FANTASY

This tall, elegant design begins with a static base of stone and sand, lightened with the wispy foliage of the whiskbroom airplant (Tillandsia juncea) and a tall feather—symbol in many cultures of wisdom, higher thought, or spiritual progression. A small, fluffy blushing bride (Tillandsia ionantha) softens the transition between the solid base and the airy, upswept feather and foliage.

1 GLASS PILSNER VASE (24 INCHES TALL)

4 CUPS PURE QUARTZ SAND

1 1/2 CUPS MONTEREY BEACH SAND

1 1/2 CUPS MONTEREY BEACH PEBBLES

3 MEDIUM CITRINE POINTS

STICK FOR POSITIONING CITRINE

1 BLUSHING BRIDE (*Tillandsia ionantha*)

1 WHISKBROOM AIRPLANT (*Tillandsia juncea*)

1 CAST-AWAY FEATHER

1. Clean terrarium glass inside and out.

2. Pour pure quartz sand into bottom quarter of the container.

3. Tip vase as if to pour a drink. While tipped, pour in Monterey beach sand and a layer of Monterey beach pebbles, then gently tilt glass back into upright position.

4. Drop in three citrine points. You can use a stick to position them in a tiny informal rock pile.

5. Place base of small blushing bride atop the citrine points, then arrange the tall whiskbroom airplant so its base is on the other side of blushing bride.

6. Finally, tuck the feather alongside the whiskbroom airplant, toward the center of the glass.

Care

Place terrarium where it will receive bright, indirect or filtered light. Avoid direct, hot midday or afternoon sun. Every 1 to 2 weeks (depending on light levels), remove airplants from terrarium and submerge in water containing quarter-strength fertilizer for 1 to 8 hours.

Tip

If your vessel's dimensions vary much from the example, you can get a general idea of how much sand and stone to add by holding your tillandsias alongside the vessel before adding any materials. Use a crayon or tape to mark how high the sand and stone will need to be for the plants to sit on top of them. You want to comfortably fit the base of the two tillandsias without having the small one look too scrunched down at the bottom of the vessel.

REMAINS OF THE DAY

47

Life and death, as we all know, are inextricably entwined. Here, embodied, is the stuff of the great cycle of life, tied together in beautiful knots and with the slow senescence of living materials completely visible before our eyes. Replace the maple samaras as they age—or don't. It's up to you.

2 HANGING GLASS TEARDROPS (6 INCHES TALL)

JUTE TWINE FOR SUSPENDING TEARDROPS

EYE-HOOK OR OTHER CEILING ATTACHMENT

3 JAPANESE MAPLE SAMARAS

1 HANDFUL CHARTREUSE REINDEER MOSS

1 SMALL HANDFUL CARNELIAN AGATE

1 SHEEP JAW BONE (FROM FAMILY FARM)

1. Clean terrarium glass inside and out.

2. Keeping string in one long length, loop each end through the eye of each glass teardrop. Secure with decorative knots, which can also be used to attach jawbone to string.

3. Add 2 maple samaras to one of the glass teardrops; in the other, place a bunch of chartreuse reindeer moss, 1 maple samara, and the carnelian agate.

Care

There's no special maintenance required for this design, as chartreuse reindeer moss is dyed and preserved and the maple samaras will gradually dry to a pale tan color. Until fresh samaras are in season again, the dried ones can be replaced with other seasonal materials such as seedpods, conifer branchlets, or cones. Or just allow the samaras to completely wither.

Tip

This design can be hung from ceiling with a stable eye-hook or other ceiling attachment. Make this terrarium on a soft surface such as a blanket, bedspread or fluffy rug—or fill the teardrops after you've secured them to the ceiling.

48

MR. CARLYLE AND THE GRUMPY BUNNY

The Scottish essayist and historian Thomas Carlyle was famously cranky. An old bound copy of his essay on romantic Scottish poet Robert Burns seems as fitting a resting place as any for a carnivorous plant known as the "angry bunny" and a slightly grouchy-looking porcelain rabbit resting—hopefully at peace—amid an array of beautiful objects.

1 BLOWN-GLASS BUBBLE BOWL (10 INCHES TALL)

6 CUPS CRUSHED LAVA ROCK

3 CUPS BLACK RIVER ROCKS

1 OLD BOOK

1 PORCELAIN "GRUMPY RABBIT" TRINKET

1 ANGRY BUNNY PLANT (*Utricularia sandersonii*)

1 PIECE OF AMMONITE (FOSSILIZED NAUTILUS SHELL)

SPRINKLING OF WHITE PEBBLES

SPRINKLING OF VINTAGE BRONZE BEADS

Tip

An experiment in temporality, this terrarium will likely disintegrate before your eyes. The soil will begin to wash down the sides; the book will gradually decompose. As long as the plant is kept continuously moist, however, it should thrive for a couple of years.

You could replace the angry bunny plant with a succulent if you tend to be forgetful about watering—this may also slow down the book's decomposition!

1. Clean terrarium glass inside and out.

2. Pour about 4 cups of crushed lava rock into base of bowl.

3. Place black river rocks over center of sand (not touching sides of container), edges up.

4. Open up old book to an appropriate page and set, spine-down on rocks. (It's nice if the book is opened toward the front of terrarium, so some words can be seen, right side up.)

5. Place porcelain rabbit (or whatever object you have chosen) at the back of bowl on the book.

6. Onto open book, pour remaining 2 cups of crushed lava rock.

7. Unpot the angry bunny plant and transfer plant with soil onto the heap of crushed lava rock.

8. Add the ammonite in a pleasing spot.

9. Drop a handful of white pebbles and vintage bronze beads near front spine of book.

Care

Angry bunny plant, a South African perennial carnivorous plant, appreciates bright, indirect light near a window. In lieu of a sunny window, try a full-spectrum fluorescent light for 18 hours a day. Keep soil moist at all times by pouring 1/4 to 1 cup of water over soil regularly and you'll be rewarded with a show of tiny white flowers. Water with distilled or rain water.

SUSPENDED IN A SUNBEAM

A delicate glass orb holds a diminutive composition of treetop treasures: a baby airplant, a few clusters of burgundy Japanese maple helicopters, and two calligraphed dove eggs in a soft nest of white sand. Two white dove feathers, suspended from vintage robin's-egg-blue string, bait your gaze to linger just a little longer.

1 HANGING BUBBLE VASE (2.5 X 3.5 INCHES)

JUTE TWINE FOR SUSPENDING VASE

EYE-HOOK OR OTHER CEILING ATTACHMENT

1 CUP PURE QUARTZ SAND

1 BUNCH JAPANESE MAPLE SAMARAS BOUND WITH STRING

2 CALLIGRAPHED DOVE EGGS

1 SMALL BLUSHING BRIDE (*Tillandsia ionantha*)

2 DOVE FEATHERS

VINTAGE BLUE STRING

1. Clean terrarium glass inside and out.

2. Attach jute twine to glass and hang before filling to make sure length is correct. It's easiest to make this terrarium if you can fill it while it's suspended. (You could also have somebody hold it for you or just rest it on a squishy down pillow).

3. Pour pure quartz sand into base and give a gentle shake.

4. Shift sand to be slightly higher in the back.

5. Nestle the Japanese maple samaras toward the back, add the blushing bride, and tuck the dove eggs in the front.

6. Attach feathers to vintage blue string and loop through the base of the glass orb.

Care

Bright, indirect or filtered light is ideal for the airplant. Avoid direct, hot midday or afternoon sun. Every 1 to 2 weeks (depending on light levels), remove the airplants from the terrarium and submerge in water containing quarter-strength fertilizer for 1 to 8 hours.

Tip

Remember that the airplant needs to be plucked out for soaking, so be sure it fits through the opening readily.

Tiny eggs can be obtained from friends with pet birds—or use speckled stones, or glass or marble eggs.

DANGLING PARTICIPLES

This lofty teardrop arrangement has the light-radiating effect of a chandelier, with the warm, reflective glass holding luminescent chartreuse moss and airy little brown and cream feathers.

7 HANGING TEARDROP VASES (6 INCHES TALL)

JUTE TWINE FOR SUSPENDING TEARDROPS

EYE-HOOKS OR OTHER CEILING ATTACHMENTS

7 CUPS HEMATITE SAND

3 CUPS CHARTREUSE REINDEER MOSS

1 HANDFUL BLACK RIVER ROCKS

A SMATTERING (10 TO 15) OF THE FOLLOWING: MAGNOLIA SEEDPODS, SPRIG OF OLD MAN'S BEARD LICHEN (*Dolichousnea longissima*), SMALL DECORATIVE BIRDS, SILK FLOWERS, BUG, PYRITE STONES, SMALL BONES, BLACK EMU FEATHER, QUARTZ CRYSTAL POINTS, WHITE PEBBLES, VINTAGE FRENCH FLOWER BEADS, MOOD MOSS (*Dicranum* species), OLD THEATER LIGHT BULB, AMETHYST CRYSTALS.

8 MINI-DECO VASES (3 INCHES TALL)

GOLD THREAD FOR SUSPENDING MINI-DECOS

15–20 SMALL HEN FEATHERS

Care

No care is required. Mood moss can be spritzed to keep it a rich green but also looks nice dried, turning a lovely honey-green.

Tip

Hang from ceiling or, better still, an existing chandelier.

1. Clean terrarium glass inside and out.

2. Thread jute twine through top loops of 7 teardrops and attach to sturdy ceiling hooks, adding a series of knots if desired.

3. Add 1 cup of hematite sand to each teardrop, as well as a bunch of chartreuse reindeer moss and a few black river rocks.

4. The rest is up to you—choose 10 to 15 pieces from the list that tickle your fancy and add them to the teardrops until you are satisfied with how they look.

5. Knot gold thread around the neck of each mini-deco vase and suspend at varying heights from sturdy ceiling hooks. To each, add 1 to 3 feathers or whatever amount most pleases you.

RESOURCES

It's wonderful to craft terrariums using what you already have or can find in nature, but it's also inspiring to get a glimpse of the wide range of available materials. This is why specialty terrarium shops are such enjoyable places to explore. Always investigate local options as well as internet sources.

Artemisia

110 SE 28th Avenue
Portland, OR 97214
503.232.8224
WWW.ARTEMISIAON28TH.COM
A wide array of terrarium making and indoor gardening supplies (including plants, mossballs, glass containers, shells, crystals, sand, stones, bones, feathers, and carved Mexican houses) as well as fine art.

The Cactus Shop

WWW.CACTUSSHOP.COM
Plants

Cedar Mountain Drums

2237 E. Burnside Street
Portland, OR 97214
503.235.6345
WWW.CEDARMOUNTAINDRUMS.COM
Antlers, shells, and feathers

Crate & Barrel

Various locations
1.800.967.6696
WWW.CRATEANDBARREL.COM
Glass

Everleaf Greens

386.527.8938
WWW.EVERLEAFGREENS.COM
Moss and lichen, mossballs

Glasshouse Works

740.662.2142
WWW.GLASSHOUSEWORKS.COM
Plants

Ikea

Various locations
WWW.IKEA.COM
Glass

Michaels

Various locations
1.800.642.4235
WWW.MICHAELS.COM
Miscellaneous crafting supplies

Miles' to Go
520.682.7272
WWW.MILES2GO.COM
Cacti and succulents

Moss Acres
1.866.438.6677
WWW.MOSSACRES.COM
Moss and lichen

Mountain Gems and Healing Crystals
877.785.5372
WWW.HEALINGCRYSTALS.NET
Crystals

The Nature Company
THENATURECOMPANY.MYBISI.COM
Shells, moss, crystals, sand, and more

Oudean's Willow Creek Nursery
7421 137th Avenue SE
Snohomish, WA 98290
360.568.6024
WWW.OUDEANSWILLOWCREEKNURSERY.COM
Carnivorous plants

Paxton Gate
824 Valencia Street
San Francisco, CA 94110
415.824.1872
WWW.PAXTONGATE.COM
Bones, bugs, and other natural materials

Pebble Tile Mosaics
1.888.444.2147
WWW.PEBBLETILEMOSAICS.COM
Stone, pebbles, and gravel

Rainforest Flora, Inc.
19121 Hawthorne Boulevard
Torrance, CA 90503
310.370.8044
WWW.RAINFORESTFLORA.COM
Plants

Sarracenia Northwest
503.630.7522
WWW.COBRAPLANT.COM
Carnivorous plants

Seashell World
1.888.515.3103
WWW.SEASHELLWORLD.COM
Shells

Shibata Floral Company
Locations in Los Angeles, San Francisco, and Portland, OR
1.888.SHIBATA
WWW.SHIBATAFC.COM
Flowers

White Flower Farm
1.800.503.9624
WWW.WHITEFLOWERFARM.COM
Plants

INDEX